HOW TO BE A
DOMESTIC GODDESS

Also by Nigella Lawson

HOW TO EAT
THE PLEASURES AND PRINCIPLES OF GOOD FOOD

NIGELLA BITES

FOREVER SUMMER

HOW TO BE A
DOMESTIC GODDESS

BAKING AND THE ART OF
COMFORT COOKING

NIGELLA LAWSON

ALFRED A. KNOPF CANADA

FOR JOHN, GODDESS-MAKER

PUBLISHED BY ALFRED A. KNOPF CANADA

Copyright © Nigella Lawson 2000
Photographs copyright © Petrina Tinslay 2000

National Library of Canada Cataloguing in Publication

Lawson, Nigella
How to be a domestic goddess : baking and the art of comfort cooking / Nigella Lawson ; photography by Petrina Tinslay. — 1st ed.

Includes bibliographical references and index.
ISBN 0-676-97410-4 (bound).—ISBN 0-676-97411-2 (pbk.)

1. Baking. 1. Cuisson au four. I. Title.

TX763.L38 2001   641.8'15   C2001-930479-X

www.randomhouse.ca

Printed and bound in Germany by
Appl Druck, Wemding

CONTENTS

PREFACE

This is a book about baking, but not a baking book – not in the sense of being a manual or a comprehensive guide or a map of a land you do not inhabit. I neither want to confine you to kitchen quarters nor even suggest that it might be desirable. But I do think that many of us have become alienated from the domestic sphere, and that it can actually make us feel better to claim back some of that space, make it comforting rather than frightening. In a way, baking stands both as a useful metaphor for the familial warmth of the kitchen we fondly imagine used to exist, and as a way of reclaiming our lost Eden. This is hardly a culinary matter, of course: but cooking, we know, has a way of cutting through things, and to things, which have nothing to do with the kitchen. This is why it matters.

The trouble with much modern cooking is not that the food it produces isn't good, but that the mood it induces in the cook is one of skin-of-the-teeth efficiency, all briskness and little pleasure. Sometimes that's the best we can manage, but at other times we don't want to feel like a post-modern, post-feminist, overstretched woman but, rather, a domestic goddess, trailing nutmeggy fumes of baking pie in our languorous wake.

So what I'm talking about is not *being* a domestic goddess exactly, but *feeling* like one. One of the reasons making cakes is satisfying is that the effort required is so much less than the gratitude conferred. Everyone seems to think it's hard to make a cake (and no need to disillusion them), but it doesn't take more than 25 minutes to make and bake a tray of muffins or a sponge layer cake, and the returns are high: you feel disproportionately good about yourself afterwards. This is what baking, what all of this book, is about: feeling good, wafting along in the warm, sweet-smelling air, unwinding, no longer being entirely an office creature; and that's exactly what I mean by 'comfort cooking'.

Part of it too is about a fond, if ironic, dream: the unexpressed 'I' that is a cross between Sophia Loren and Debbie Reynolds in pink cashmere cardigan and fetching gingham pinny, a weekend alter-ego winning adoring glances and endless approbation from anyone who has the good fortune to eat in her kitchen. The good thing is, we don't have to get ourselves up in Little Lady drag and we don't have to renounce the world and enter into a life of domestic drudgery. But we can bake a little – and a cake is just a cake, far easier than getting the timing right for even the most artlessly casual of midweek dinner parties.

This isn't a dream; what's more, it isn't even a nightmare.

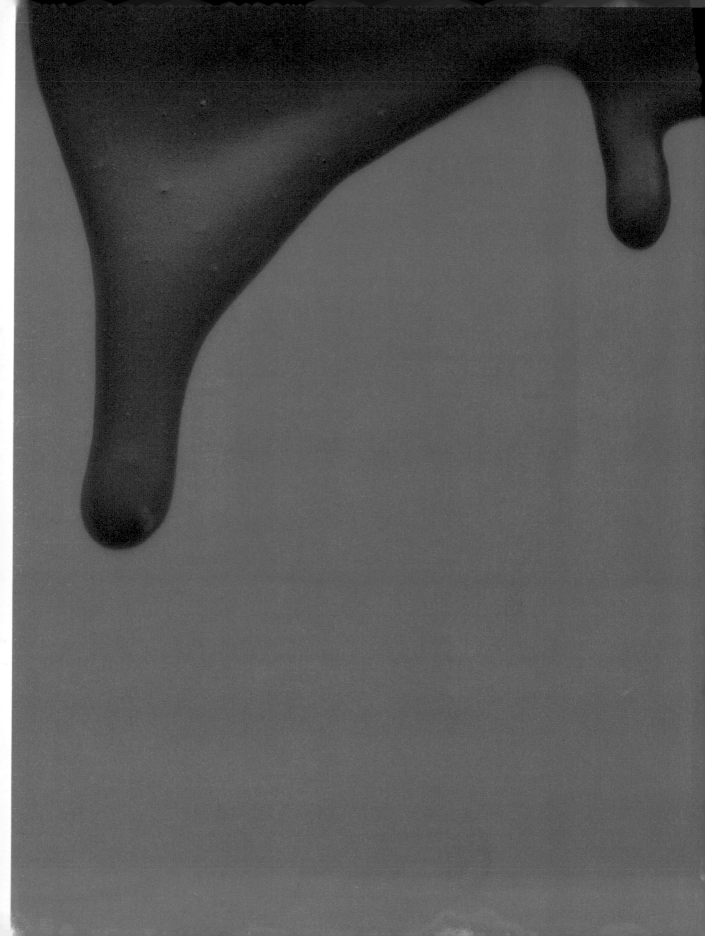

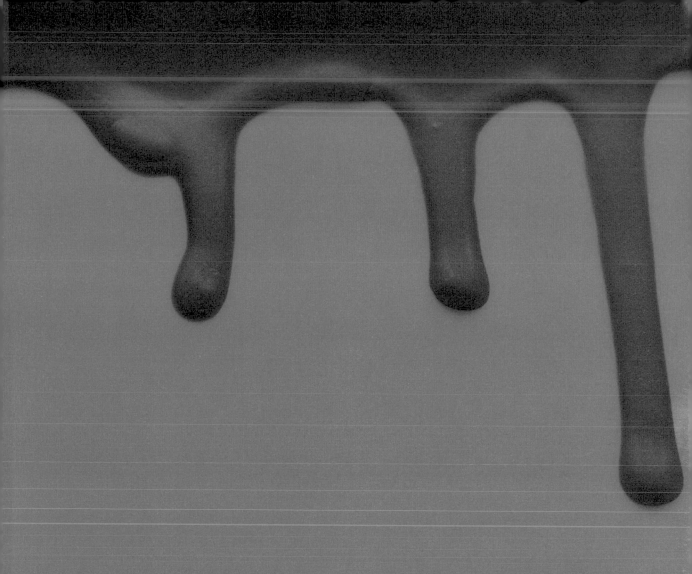

CAKES

CAKES

Cake baking has to be, however innocently, one of the great culinary scams: it implies effort, it implies domestic prowess; but believe me, it's easy. We've become so convinced that simple food comes out of simple cooking that we're happy to cook elaborate Tuscan suppers – which in reality demand much more than we could ever believe possible – but then baulk at baking a cake, assuming that we don't have the time for all that, that we live a life that doesn't encompass those arcane culinary arts.

If that's how you think, then you're wrong. You know how you make a cake? You mix a few basic ingredients together, stick the mixture in a tin and bake it. And when I say mix, I don't mean mix it yourself, not if you don't want to: I mean process or beat with an electric mixer. How hard can that be?

Too much reassurance can, I know, be troubling in itself. If it's so easy to bake a cake, why is it that you can't? Be honest: I imagine the answer is that you don't often try, or haven't for years. Not all cakes come out perfectly or even the same each time, and not all cakes are equally easy to bake, but if you follow any one of the recipes below, you can be sure it will work. Of course there are always variants in cooking, some more controllable than others, but baking is somewhat different: it's chemistry first, poetry second. That's partly why I came to it late. When you're making a stew, well, you can go your own way, follow instinct, taste, convenience; you couldn't make a cake like this: a cake demands mathematical respect.

Some rules extend beyond the confines of the individual texts. You must remember three basic things: the first is that all ingredients should be at room temperature when you start; the second is that the oven should be at the required temperature when you put in the filled tin; finally, that tin should be of the dimensions specified. (If I'm honest, you can get away with some deviation here, but not too much – and anyway, why make things harder for yourself?)

I've said it's easy to make a cake, but this doesn't convey the depth of achievement you feel on making one. There's something about seeing such elemental change, that flour, butter, eggs, sugar could become this – and more, that you've brought it about – that's so satisfying. Such simple pleasures are not to be underestimated.

LOAF AND PLAIN CAKES

This is baking at its simplest and most elegant. There's no folderol or fancy footwork: you just feel humble and worthy and brimming with good things.

MY MOTHER-IN-LAW'S MADEIRA CAKE

I don't know if I ever ate Madeira cake as a child, but just the sight of this golden-yellow loaf with its long crack down the middle makes me feel satisfactorily nostalgic. This recipe, given to me by my mother-in-law Carrie, is the best of any version I've tried. It's just one of those plain cakes you think you can't see the point of, until you start slicing and eating it.

240g softened unsalted butter
200g caster sugar, plus extra for sprinkling
grated zest and juice of 1 lemon

3 large eggs
210g self-raising flour
90g plain flour
23 x 13 x 7cm loaf tin, buttered and lined

Preheat the oven to 170°C/gas mark 3.

Cream the butter and sugar, and add the lemon zest. Add the eggs one at a time with a tablespoon of the flour for each. Then gently mix in the rest of the flour and, finally, the lemon juice. Sprinkle with caster sugar (about 2 tablespoons should do it) as it goes into the oven, and bake for 1 hour or until a cake-tester comes out clean. Remove to a wire rack, and let cool in the tin before turning out.

Makes 8–10 slices.

VARIATION

I love a good old-fashioned seed cake; if you do too, add a couple of teaspoons of caraway to this mixture. For a lemon poppyseed cake, add the juice of another half lemon and a tablespoon or two of poppyseeds. And I once came across an expensive but tempting curiosity: dried strawberries, tiny things harvested by that clever Terence Conran. I upped the liquid to the juice of 2 lemons and folded in 100g of the strawberries. It was a wholly successful experiment.

EASY ALMOND CAKE

This cake isn't baked in a loaf tin but in a ring mould, preferably a patterned one; and it's a plain cake only in the sense that it isn't filled or iced (though feel free). It's densely almondy and eggily intense. And you know how you make it? You buy a block of ready-made marzipan and put it in the processor along with eggs, flour, sugar, butter and a sprinkle of extracts and blitz.

You could easily use a plain cake tin for this cake but I always use my Springform tube pan (not hard to find) because the particular scent and delicacy of this cake makes it perfect as a dinner-party pudding with a few raspberries in the middle, a few more scattered around the edge and a light dusting of icing powder. When we cooked it for the picture opposite, we couldn't find the right tin (losing essential items is something of a speciality of mine), plus some of it stuck to the tin we did use. I could have cooked it again, but I didn't want to, because these things happen to all of us and I wanted to show it wasn't the end of the world. True, you don't see the moulding as well as you might, if at all, but a quick bit of patching and some judicial sieve-work with icing sugar and it looked fine. Life isn't lived in a lab.

One gentle reminder here: you just will not get the marzipan to ooze into the cake batter if it starts off fridge-cold. In dire straits, I have cubed it and given it a quick whirl in the microwave. And if you wanted to replace the vanilla extract with the zest of an orange, I wouldn't mind in the slightest.

250g softened unsalted butter
250g softened marzipan
150g caster sugar
¼ teaspoon almond essence
¼ teaspoon vanilla extract

6 large eggs
150g self-raising flour
25cm Springform tube pan or
    patterned ring mould, buttered
    and floured

Preheat oven to 170°C/gas mark 3. Chop the butter and marzipan to make them easier to break down, and put them in the bowl of the food processor, fitted with the double-bladed knife, with the sugar. Process until combined and pretty well smooth. Add almond essence and vanilla extract, process again, then break the eggs one at a time through the funnel, processing again each time. Tip the flour down the funnel, processing yet again, and then pour the mixture into the prepared tin, scraping the sides and bottom with a rubber spatula.

Bake for 50 minutes, but check from 40. Then, when the cake looks golden and cooked and a cake-tester or fine skewer (or a piece of spaghetti) comes out cleanish, remove from the oven and leave to cool in the tin before turning out. (This is when you will be feeling grateful if it's the Springform you're using.)

The fact that you could easily get 12 slices out of this is another reason why it comes in useful when you've got people coming for dinner. That it keeps for a good week is another point in its favour; you don't have to be fiddling around with all the courses just before lift-off. And if you don't want to eat raspberries with it, like the rosemary cake it's very good with apples. With this cake, I make a glorious pink apple purée. Either go for apples stewed in blood-orange juice (wonderful around February when the tarocchi are in) which gives a tenderly coral tint, adding a cinnamon stick or $1/2$–1 teaspoon of ground cinnamon, or use red-skinned eating apples and don't peel them before cooking them. In fact, there's no need to core them either, just chop the apples roughly and put them in a pan with some butter, lemon juice, cinnamon or cloves and, if there's some around, a slug of Calvados. Sieve the apples when they're cooked to an utterly yielding pulp, or push them through a food mill. If you want to smarten up the cake-plus-purée deal, then provide a bowl of crème fraîche (with or without Calvados and a little golden icing sugar stirred in) with some toasted flaked almonds on top.

I am not someone who enjoys peeling and depithing oranges at great length, but sliced tarocchi, or ordinary oranges, with a syrup made by reducing equal volumes of juice and sugar to an almost-caramel, would partner an orange-zested version of this almond ring (the zest in place of vanilla) exquisitely.

Needless to say, I also love this cake with a bowl of new season's rhubarb on the side, cooked as if for the rhubarb tart (see p107). And just one further suggestion . . . ice it with chocolate ganache (see p22) or just top with it at the moment of serving so it's still warm and thickly runny, and serve with a bowl of vanilla ice cream with cooled, toasted, flaked almonds sprinkled over (and I suppose you could actually spoon the ice cream into the central cavity, before drizzling over the chocolate ganache and sprinkling over these almonds).

The point of these suggestions is not simply to be interfering and bossy, but to show how cake-baking, which one ordinarily associates with the sort of teas no one eats any more, can be brought to the service of contemporary eating. To call this book 'Baking and the Dinner Party Solution' would not to be too far-fetched. In fact, I will return to this theme later – and see p39.

Serves 10–12.

ROSEMARY LOAF CAKE

In build, this is much the same as the Madeira cake, but it tastes very different. Don't be alarmed at the idea of using a herb usually associated with savoury cooking: there is something muskily aromatic about it against the sweet vanilla egginess of the cake. And the cake itself works extraordinarily well as part of an elegantly austere pudding. I love it sliced thickly and eaten with cold, stewed apples. Peel, core and chop 3 or 4 large cooking apples, squeeze over the juice of a lemon and an orange, sprinkle with sugar to taste (I'd start off with 2 tablespoons per apple and be prepared to double it) and add a knob of butter. Cook till the fruit is pale and pulpy and leave to cool. If you want to point up the flavours, you could always chuck in a small sprig of rosemary, which you should remove when you're decanting the cold almost-purée to a bowl; but go steadily, we're aiming for subtlety here. I use my stash of rosemary sugar for sprinkling over this cake (just because it's there, really – and see p336) but you can replace it with ordinary or golden caster sugar without a second thought.

250g soft unsalted butter
200g golden caster sugar
3 large eggs
210g self-raising flour
90g plain flour
1 teaspoon vanilla extract

needles from a 10cm stalk of
    rosemary, chopped small, but not
    too fine (about 2 teaspoons)
4 tablespoons milk
1–2 tablespoons rosemary sugar or
    golden caster sugar
23 x 13 x 7cm loaf tin, buttered and
    lined

Preheat the oven to 170°C/gas mark 3. Now cream the butter, adding the sugar when it's really soft, and creaming both together till pale and smooth and light. Beat in the eggs one at a time, folding in a spoonful of the flour after each addition, then add the vanilla. Fold in the rest of the flour – I find a rubber spatula the best tool for the job – and finally the rosemary. Thin the batter with the milk – you're after a soft, dropping consistency – and pour, with some helpful prodding and scraping with your spatula, into the waiting tin. Sprinkle the top with a little sugar before putting it in the oven, and cook for 1 hour, or until a cake-tester comes out clean. Leave to cool on a wire rack, in its tin, and when completely cold, unmould and wrap well in foil till you need to eat it. Like all these sorts of cakes, it keeps well.

Serves 8–10.

GATEAU BRETON

I came across this recipe for Brittany butter cake in the wonderful Anne Willan's *Real Food*, and as she says, it's really a cross between shortbread and pound cake. Rather like the crostata on p105, it's hard to decide whether it's cake or pastry. I love a stubby slice of this any time, but it does make a perfect, chic ending to a dinner party, too, either with ice cream or fruit, or if you've already had cheese, just with the coffee that follows.

Anne Willan suggests a kneading motion to bring this very sticky dough into shape; I use the dough hook on my free-standing mixer.

Use the best butter that you can find, for this is the plain cake at its simple best, and the taste of each of these few ingredients is crucial.

for the cake:

225g plain flour, preferably Italian 00
250g caster sugar
250g unsalted butter, cut into cubes
6 large egg yolks

25cm Springform tin, buttered well

for the glaze:

1 teaspoon of egg yolk, from your 6
1 tablespoon of water

Preheat the oven to 190°C/gas mark 5. Mix the glaze, and put aside while you get on with your gateau.

Put the flour into a bowl (I never bother to sieve 00 flour because it's so finely milled, but if you're using regular plain flour then do so), stir in the sugar and add the butter and egg yolks.

With the dough-hook attachment of a mixer, slowly whirr till you've got a smooth, golden dough. (If you're making this by hand, make a mound of the flour on a worktop, then make a well in it and add the sugar, butter and eggs and knead to mix.) Scoop this dough into the tin, and smooth the top with a floured hand: expect it to be very sticky; indeed, it should be.

Brush the gateau with the glaze, and mark a lattice design on top with the prongs of a fork. For a reason I am not technically proficient enough to explain, sometimes the tine marks leave a firm, striated imprint (a bit like the scrapy lines that drive Gregory Peck mad in *Spellbound*); at others, as with the cake in the picture, they barely show once the cake's cooked. Bake for 15 minutes, then turn the oven down to 180°C/gas mark 4 and give it another 25 minutes or so until it's golden on top and firm to the touch.

Let it cool completely in the tin before unmoulding it. It'll keep well if you've got a reliably airtight tin. When you come to eat it, either cut it in traditional – though slightly narrower – cake-like wedges or, as I prefer if I'm eating it at the end of dinner, criss-cross, making irregularly sized diamonds.

Serves 8–10.

1 lemon and its juice, leaving out the milk, or using the scantest amount if necessary.

There are another two fruity variants I play with. One is a rhubarb version, another a passionfruit one. In both cases, I use a teaspoonful of Boyajian orange oil in the cake. For the rhubarb filling, I stew about 500g rhubarb (or a 400g packet of the cut-down stalks) either using the poaching method (see p107) or with about 100g of sugar and the juice of half an orange in a saucepan on the hob. Since I don't mind if this goes pulpy, I generally go for the stove-top method. Sieve, reserving the juice. When the rhubarb is neither too soggy nor too warm, spread it over one of the cakes and add whipped cream. Reduce the rhubarb juice to an intense syrup, let it cool slightly, and drizzle over the cream. Then sit the second cake on top and sprinkle with caster sugar as usual.

With the passionfruit version, I make a passionfruit fool to lie softly in the middle of the sponge sandwich and a passionfruit glaze to dribble over the top. Mix the spooned-out pulp (seeds and all) of 4 passionfruit with the juice of a scant half lemon and a squeeze of orange, and set aside while you whisk about 100ml double cream with 30g sieved icing sugar till it's forming soft peaks. Just before serving, fold the passionfruit mixture into the cream and scrape it onto the top of one of the cakes. Lightly arrange the second cake over the filling and get on with the glaze. Push the pulp of another 4 passionfruit through a sieve and add to this aromatic liquid the juice of half an orange. Mix to a runny paste with sieved icing sugar – start with 100g and add more orange juice or more sugar as required. Pour over the waiting cake, letting it drip down the sides – I just drizzle it back and forth across the top, and let it run where it will.

For a coffee sandwich, keep the vanilla extract but add, too, 1 tablespoon of instant espresso powder to the flour in the cake mix. Fill with coffee buttercream (see p210, but use espresso powder instead of vanilla) and if you really want to go to town, make double the buttercream, spread it slightly thinner for the filling and use the rest to coat the sides and top of the sandwich, covering the top, or indeed the whole thing, with walnut halves.

Other ideas you might want to bear in mind include the lemon variant of the sponge filled with poached dried apricots or baked plums and crème fraîche – though we're moving into Boston cream pie territory here – or the vanilla version filled with prunes that have been soaked then cooked in Armagnac, placed on one of the cakes, then covered with a crème patissière (see p22) that has been flavoured with brandy rather than vanilla. And when gooseberries are in brief season, stew 100–150g with 1–2 tablespoons of sugar, 1 tablespoon of butter and a couple of tablespoons of elderflower cordial (or, if you've got access to some, a couple of heads of elderflower, which you remove before mushing), then fork to a rough purée. When cool, fold into some softly whipped cream (you're making a gooseberry fool comparable to the passionfruit fool above) and fill a cake which you've made using a tablespoonful of elderflower cordial in place of vanilla. Strictly speaking, you should reduce the sugar to compensate for the sweetness of the cordial, but I like to leave the filling tart, so don't worry too much about the sugariness of the cake.

Boston cream pie

Butterscotch layer cake

Flora's famous courgette cake

Victoria sponge

AUTUMNAL BIRTHDAY CAKE

There is no reason on earth why this, adapted from the *Magnolia Bakery Cookbook*, has to be a birthday cake, but since the first two times I made it were for my sister-in-law's and a friend's birthdays in late October and early November, that's how I think of it. In both cases, I put just one (gold) candle on top: better on any number of counts. I know that adorning plates with autumn leaves is not my usual aesthetic, but that's another benefit of using this as a birthday cake: you can allow yourself a little ironic leeway.

for the cake:
175g butter, softened
100g golden caster sugar
3 large eggs
350ml maple syrup
500g self-raising flour
175ml hot water
2 x 21cm sandwich tins, buttered and lined

for the icing:
2 large egg whites
125ml maple syrup
125g golden caster sugar
¹/₄ teaspoon cream of tartar
¹/₄ teaspoon salt
1 teaspoon vanilla extract
¹/₄ teaspoon maple extract, optional
125g pecans

Preheat the oven to 180°C/gas mark 4.

Beat together the butter and sugar until very pale and fluffy. Add the eggs one at a time, beating in well after each addition, then gradually add the maple syrup to make a smooth mixture. Finally, spoon in the flour alternately with the hot water, beating gently until smooth again. Divide the batter between the two tins, and cook for 40 minutes. A cake-tester, inserted, should come out clean when they're cooked. Let the cakes cool in their tins on a rack for 10 minutes before unmoulding them, then leave them to get cold before you get on with the icing.

Put everything except the pecans and extracts into a glass or metal bowl that fits over a saucepan to form a double boiler. Fill the saucepan with enough water to come just below – but not touching – the bowl when it sits on top. Bring the water to the boil, set the bowl on top and, using an electric hand-held whisk, beat the mixture vigorously for 5–7 minutes. It should stand up in peaks like a meringue mixture. Take the bowl off the saucepan, away from the heat, and add the extracts, beating them in for another minute.

Cut out 4 strips of baking parchment and use to line the cake plate, as explained on p22. Using your dreamy, ivory-coloured meringue, ice the middle, sides and top of the cake. Give the icing a swirly effect rather than smooth, letting the top have small peaks. Chop most of the pecans finely, leaving some pieces larger. Sprinkle over the top of the cake, and throw at the sides.

This cake is best eaten the day it's cooked.

Serves 8.

BABY BUNDTS

At a blackboard-walled vegetarian café in New York once, I ate a little yoghurty lemony ring-moulded cake and wanted to whip up something similar immediately on my return. I've given you this version not simply because it reminds me of the original inspirational one I ate but because it's the simplest to make. Melting the butter and then proceeding simply by stirring wet ingredients into dry (rather than rubbing butter into flour and so forth) won it for me.

It's getting easier and easier to buy what might once have been recherché baking materials, so I don't feel guilty about suggesting a recipe that requires a tray of mini-Bundt moulds; but if you anticipate problems finding one, see pviii.

for the cakes:
125ml natural (preferably bio) yoghurt
75g butter, melted
2 large eggs
zest of 1 lemon
150g plain flour
1/2 teaspoon bicarbonate of soda
pinch of salt

125g caster sugar
1 mini-Bundt tray with 6 moulds,
approximately 9 x 41/2cm each,
buttered or oiled well

for the icing:
200g icing sugar
juice of 1 lemon

Preheat the oven to 170°C/gas mark 3.

In a measuring jug, mix the yoghurt, melted butter, eggs and lemon zest. Put the flour, bicarb, salt and sugar into a large bowl. Mix the wet ingredients into the bowl, folding everything in well, then fill the mini-Bundt moulds with the mixture, and cook for 25–30 minutes. When they come out of the oven, leave them to cool a little before turning them out, otherwise they'll break – but don't let them get too cold either, as they will stick. Let them cool on a rack, flat-side down.

To make the icing, sieve the icing sugar into a bowl, and add enough lemon juice to make an icing thick enough to ice the tops and drizzle down like snow-capped peaks.

Makes 6.

VARIATION

As with all citrus recipes, you can be fairly free with substitutions. Lime is an obvious and beckoning proposition. And you could use orange either as an alternative or along with the lemon (say the zest and juice of a half of each for the cakes and icing respectively) to make a St Clement's version.

FRUITED CAKES

I haven't gone all quaint and ye olde. I use the word 'fruited' simply to make it clear that what follows is not just fruit cakes – in fact, there's only one here – but all sorts of cakes with fruit in them. For the rest of the more traditional fruit cakes, turn to the Christmas chapter.

CHERRY-ALMOND LOAF CAKE

I have a nostalgic fondness for this yellow slab punctured by waxy halves of scarlet cherries – the cake we called station cake at home – but this is best with those dark and glossy natural-coloured glacé cherries.

200g natural-coloured glacé cherries
250g self-raising flour
225g butter, softened
175g caster sugar
3 large eggs, beaten

2–3 drops almond essence
100g ground almonds
6 tablespoons milk
23 x 13 x 7cm loaf tin, lined and
   buttered

Preheat the oven to 170°C/gas mark 3. Halve the cherries, wash them in a colander under cold water, then pat them dry, toss them in some flour and shake well to get rid of excess.

Cream the butter and sugar until light and fluffy. Gradually add the beaten eggs and almond essence, then gently fold in the flour and ground almonds. Fold in the cherries and then the milk and spoon the thick mixture into the loaf tin and bake for ¾–1 hour, or until a cake-tester comes out clean.

As with all of these sorts of cakes, leave in the tin on a wire rack until completely cooled.

Makes 8–10 slices.

BANANA BREAD

This is the first recipe anyone hesitant about baking should try: it's fabulously easy and fills the kitchen with that aromatic fug which is the natural atmospheric setting for the domestic goddess. There are countless recipes for banana bread: this one is adapted from one of my favourite books, the one I read lying on the sofa to recover from yet another long, modern, stressed-out day, Jim Fobel's *Old-Fashioned Baking Book: Recipes from an American Childhood*. If you're thinking about giving this cake to children, don't worry, the alcohol doesn't pervade: you just end up with stickily, aromatically swollen fruit.

100g sultanas

75ml bourbon or dark rum

175g plain flour

2 teaspoons baking powder

1/2 teaspoon bicarbonate of soda

1/2 teaspoon salt

125g unsalted butter, melted

150g sugar

2 large eggs

4 small, very ripe bananas (about 300g weighed without skin), mashed

60g chopped walnuts

1 teaspoon vanilla extract

23 x 13 x 7cm loaf tin, buttered and floured or with a paper insert

Put the sultanas and rum or bourbon in a smallish saucepan and bring to the boil. Remove from the heat, cover and leave for an hour if you can, or until the sultanas have absorbed most of the liquid, then drain.

Preheat the oven to 170°C/gas mark 3 and get started on the rest. Put the flour, baking powder, bicarb and salt in a medium-sized bowl and, using your hands or a wooden spoon, combine well. In a large bowl, mix the melted butter and sugar and beat until blended. Beat in the eggs one at a time, then the mashed bananas. Then, with your wooden spoon, stir in the walnuts, drained sultanas and vanilla extract. Add the flour mixture, a third at a time, stirring well after each bit. Scrape into the loaf tin and bake in the middle of the oven for 1–1¼ hours. When it's ready, an inserted toothpick or fine skewer should come out cleanish. Leave in the tin on a rack to cool, and eat thickly or thinly sliced, as you prefer.

Makes 8–10 slices.

VARIATION

I haven't done a tremendous amount of fiddling with this, but I did once make it, for friends who are more chocolate-crazed than I am, by replacing 25g of the flour with good cocoa powder (not drinking chocolate) and adding 100g of dark chocolate, cut up into smallish chunks. And you could just as easily use the chocolate chips sold in the baking aisle of supermarkets.

MARZIPAN FRUIT CAKE

This may be the only proper fruit cake in this section, but it is my favourite one in the entire world. This is in the first place because it contains marzipan (which I love) and in the second because it doesn't contain any peel (which I hate, or do in its normal, bitter, shop-bought state). Moreover, the dried pears which I've thrown in as well have a fudgy graininess which melds perfectly with the marzipan.

You do have to start this the night before you're baking, but all that means is the marzipan needs chopping and freezing and the fruits need soaking in advance.

150g sultanas
100g natural-coloured glacé cherries, halved
150g dried pears, chopped
100ml white rum
250g marzipan
50g ground almonds
zest of 1 lemon
175g plain flour

100g caster sugar
100g butter
2 large eggs
1 teaspoon orange-flower water
20cm Springform cake tin, buttered and lined bottom and sides, so that the parchment comes a good 10cm above the rim.

So, the night before, mix the sultanas, glacé cherries and pears in a large bowl and cover with the rum. Dice the marzipan and put in the freezer. Leave both to soak and freeze overnight.

When you come to make the cake the next day, preheat the oven to 140°C/gas mark 1. Beat together the almonds, lemon zest, flour, sugar, butter and eggs. Add the drained fruit, orange-flower water and the frozen marzipan. Put the cake mix into the tin, levelling the surface and making a slight indent in the middle to get an even surface when cooked. Bake for 2–2$\frac{1}{2}$ hours or until a cake-tester comes out clean. Don't overcook, as it will continue to cook in its own warmth as it cools. But nor should you worry too much about it: there's enough fruit and marzipanny squidge to make sure this golden cake doesn't easily turn dry.

Allow the cake to cool in the tin before rewrapping in parchment and foil to store for about a week. Feed with a little more rum before you wrap for a richer taste if you want (just puncture the top of the cake a few times and slowly dribble a few spoons of rum over). You should also be aware that the wrap-and-keep advice is a counsel of perfection. Last time I made this, two days was the longest I was able to leave it before greedily unwrapping and slicing into it.

Serves 8–10.

CUPCAKES

Now this really is 'Baking and the Dinner Party Solution'.

At about the time I started getting into top cupcake and fairy-cake mode, ostensibly for children, I noticed that the people who really seemed to get excited by them were the children's parents. I think it's not till you hit 30 that nostalgia is even a remotely comforting option. Since then, I've decided that cupcakes and fairy cakes – by which I mean the plain-bottomed prettily iced cupcakes – are the perfect things to make for dinner. And by this I mean not some shiny tabled, silver-laid grand dinner party but those evenings when you have friends for supper in the kitchen (the only kind of dinner party I know). Give people cheese instead of pudding (or nothing at all: it ain't obligatory) and wheel out these dinky numbers with the coffee and tea. You can make the cakes a day in advance, keep them in an airtight container and ice them later – although since the icing helps keep them fresh you may as well, if you're using a water rather than a butter icing, ice them a day before too and then you'll have nothing to do on the day itself.

I don't normally like teensy-weensy individually portioned things, but cupcakes seem to hit some pre-rational spot and I succumb. But then everyone always does. What follows is not all there is: see also cappuccino and espresso cupcakes on pp198-9, chocolate-cherry cupcakes on p196, dolly-mixture fairy cakes on p215, butterfly cakes on p217, Halloween cupcakes on p216 and Christmas cupcakes on p267.

FAIRY CAKES

These are so quick both to make and to bake that it really is possible to whip some up for after dinner when you get home from work. On the whole, I leave my fairy cakes plain and unadorned beneath; it's above, when I get to play with colours and flowers and sugar decorations, that a little imagination and artistry comes into play. Not that I can claim much credit, certainly not for the latter: I buy rice-paper roses and sugar daisies and pansies rather than make them. But I like the playing part – choosing the colours, the detail. My weak spot is the white-on-white look. (In fact, I've told Hettie, my saviour and right-hand, who's worked with me since this book's inception, that when she gets married she has to let me make her a stacked pyramid of these. Luckily, she's up for it.)

My other favourite – and then I really will leave you to your own devices – is the fifties pistachio-green version (Colourway's food-colouring paste in 'Gooseberry') with the pale-pink rice-paper rose atop.

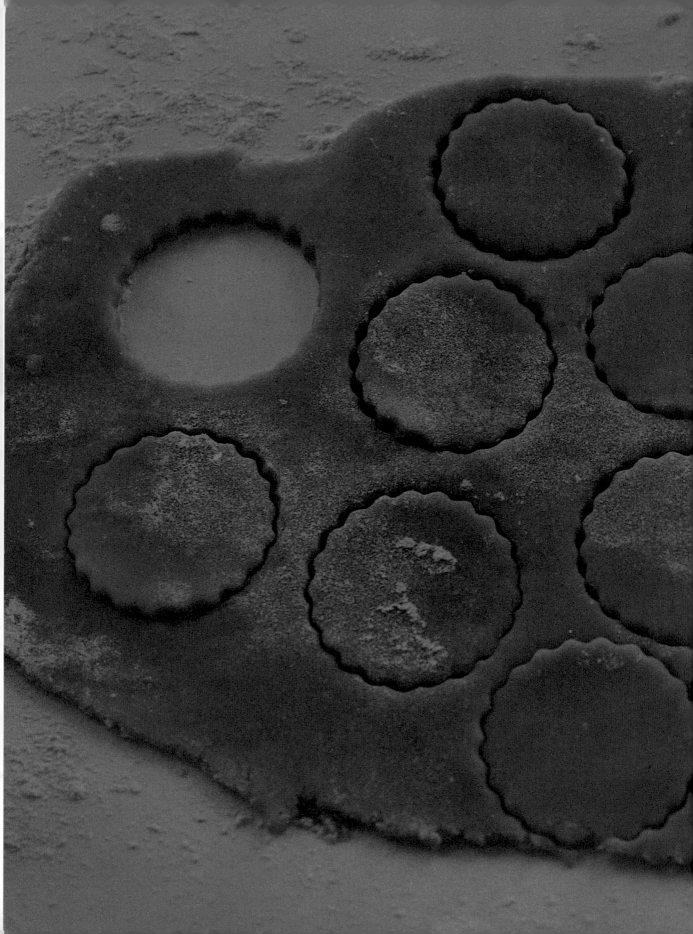

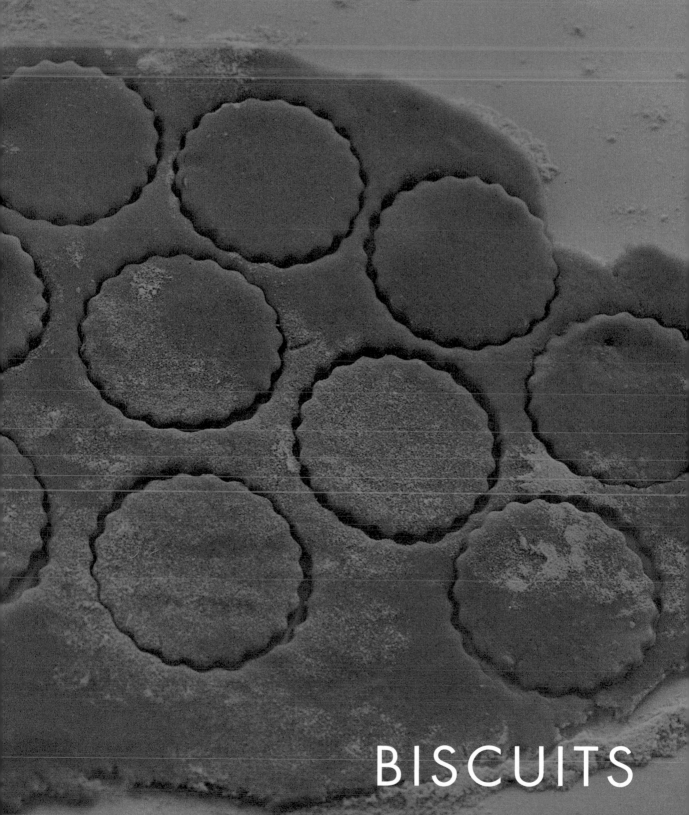

BISCUITS

BISCUITS

Including Scones, Muffins, Pancakes and Small Things

Biscuits are one of the first things we learn to cook when we're little – or at least roll and stamp out, get the feel of, which is just as important – and there seems to be a sense in which we're recapturing some remembered, no doubt idealized, past whenever we make them in adulthood; they still feel like playing. When I want to cook but have no fixed idea of what, and have no actual meal to prepare to justify fiddling about in the kitchen, I often convince myself that there are biscuits that need to be made.

The biscuits here are mostly of the free-form kind: you either spoon them onto a tray or roll them into balls between your hands to shape them. There are exceptions, as you'll see, but the blueprint recipe for cutter-shaped biscuits is in the children's chapter. Their need, I felt, was greater than ours. (And, of course, for chocolate biscuits, see the chocolate chapter.)

I know biscuit-baking may seem a quaintly archaic practice now, but it can make a modern life very much easier. A lot of the recipes that follow can be made to augment a tub of good, bought ice cream to ridiculously great effect. And much easier than making the ice cream and buying the biscuits.

ROSEBUD MADELEINES

It was the curled-in smallness of these tender sponge biscuits, as well as the fact that they're flavoured with rosewater, that made me name them as I have. I like them with coffee when pudding's been just a plate of cheese, but eat them with whatever and however you want. The dried rosebuds in the picture are obviously not an obligatory ingredient: for me, it's just a *Citizen Kane* kinda thing.

**50g unsalted butter, plus 1 tablespoon
    for greasing
1 large egg
40g caster sugar
pinch of salt**

**45g plain flour, preferably Italian 00
1 tablespoon rosewater
icing sugar for dusting
24-bun mini-madeleine tin**

Melt all the butter over a low heat, then leave to cool. Beat the egg, caster sugar and salt in a bowl for about 5 minutes, preferably with an electric mixer of some sort, until it's as thick as mayonnaise. Then sprinkle in the flour; I hold a sieve above the egg and sugar mixture, put the flour in and shake it through. Fold in the flour with a wooden spoon and then set aside a scant tablespoon of the cold, melted butter for greasing the tins and fold in the rest along with the rosewater. Mix well, but not too vigorously. Leave to rest in the fridge for 1 hour, then take out and leave at room temperature for half an hour. Preheat the oven to 220°C/gas mark 7.

Generously brush the insides of the madeleine tins with the tablespoon of butter (melting more if you feel you need it) before filling them with half the cake mixture (this amount does 2 batches). About 1 teaspoonful in each should do: don't worry about covering the moulded indentations; in the heat of the oven the mixture will spread before it rises. Bake for 5 minutes, though check after 3. Turn out and let cool on a rack, then arrange on a plate and dust with icing sugar. Repeat with the remaining half of the mixture.

Makes 48.

COCONUT MACAROONS

These are a very English kind of macaroon, the sort you always used to see displayed in bakers' shops alongside the madelines (those sponge castles dipped in luminous strawberry jam and dredged in throat-catching dessiccated coconut, and so very different from those that inflamed the memory of Marcel Proust). The difference with coconut macaroons is that you need neither to be ironic nor self-consciously retro-cool to enjoy them.

One bit of retail bossiness here: buy shredded, not dessiccated, coconut, otherwise the sugary, fragrant dampness – which is, after all, the whole point – will be lost.

2 large egg whites
¼ teaspoon cream of tartar
100g caster sugar
30g ground almonds
pinch of salt

1 teaspoon vanilla extract
(or coconut essence, should such be available)
250g shredded coconut
1 baking sheet, lined

Preheat the oven to 170°C/gas mark 3.

Beat the egg whites until frothy – no more – then add the cream of tartar and carry on beating, Missus, until soft peaks are formed. Add the sugar a teaspoon at a time and whisk until the peaks can hold their shape and are shiny. Fold in the almonds, salt, vanilla and coconut. The mixture will be sticky but should, all the same, hold its shape when clumped together.

Form into clementine-sized domes, 6–7cm in diameter. Don't make them too flat; they look best if you keep them nicely rounded, but this is really just a matter of personal taste, so follow your own.

Cook for 20 minutes or until they're just beginning to turn golden in parts.

Makes 8 large macaroons.

PISTACHIO MACAROONS

These are the world's most elegant macaroons. The colour alone, that waxy pale jade, perfectly matches the aromatic delicacy of their taste; and their nutty chewiness melts into the fragrant, soft paste with which they're paired. Of all the recipes in this book, this is the one of which I think I'm most proud: biscuit bliss.

These are perfect at the end of dinner alongside some icing-sugar-dusted raspberries; or alone with coffee, gracefully piled on a plate or cake stand.

for the macaroons:
75g pistachios
125g icing sugar
2 large egg whites
15g caster sugar

for the buttercream:
55g pistachios
250g icing sugar
125g unsalted butter, softened
2 baking sheets, lined

Preheat the oven to 180°C/gas mark 4.

Grind the pistachios in a food processor along with the icing sugar (this stops them turning into an oily mess), until as fine as dust. Whisk the egg whites until fairly stiff, but not dry, sprinkle the caster sugar over and whisk until very stiff. Fold the whites into the pistachio-sugar dust, and combine gently. Pipe small rounds onto your lined baking sheet, using a plain 1cm nozzle. Let them sit for about 10 minutes to form a skin. Then put in the oven and cook for 10–12 minutes: they should be set, but not dried out.

Remove from the oven and let cool, still on their sheets, while you get on with the filling. This is simple work: grind the nuts and icing sugar in the processor as before; then cream the butter and continue creaming as you add the nut dust. Make sure you have a well-combined soft buttercream. Then simply sandwich the macaroons together.

Makes 20, i.e., 40 sandwiched together.

SPANISH MACAROONS

I'm not sure I would spend a whole lot of time trying to persuade a Spaniard of the origin of these biscuits, but I call them Spanish because they seem so instantly redolent of that aroma of oranges, almonds and the faintest warm breath of cinnamon that I associate with Spain. Indeed, I have a vague taste-memory of eating macaroons like this when I was in Seville once, and I suppose it was those that I was trying to recreate. I know in my heart of hearts they would be better with blanched almonds which you then grind yourself when you want them, but since I made these with ready-ground nuts and was pleased with them as they were, it seemed honest to leave it that way. If you decide to buy whole almonds to grind, get 500g: they're oilier than the ready-ground, so you need more to get the right consistency.

425g ready-ground or 500g whole blanched almonds, ground
250g icing sugar, sieved
zest of 2 oranges

1/2 teaspoon almond essence
1/2 teaspoon cinnamon
1 large egg, plus 3 large egg whites
2 baking trays, lined

Preheat the oven to 180°C/gas mark 4.

Mix together the almonds, icing sugar, orange zest, almond essence and cinnamon. In a separate bowl, or wide-mouthed measuring jug, beat the whole egg together with the egg whites. Make a well in the centre of your dry ingredients, then pour and mix in the egg. The mixture will be very sticky, I know, but that's fine.

Form walnut-sized balls by rolling the torn-off pieces of dough between your palms, and place on the prepared baking sheets. It will help if you wet your hands under a cold tap and go back to the sink for degunging and rewetting every now and again as you go along. Apart from making the whole operation less messy, it will make for smoother biscuits.

Cook for 20 minutes, by which time the biscuits should look lightly browned on the surface but won't have lost their sweet and tender chewiness underneath. Cool on a rack.

Makes about 30.

SWEET AND SALTY PEANUT BISCUITS

If greed alone were the spur and measure, these would be my favourite biscuits. There's something about the contrast between salt and sweet and their crumbly lightness that makes them instantly addictive. They make a seductive partnership with vanilla ice cream: you can do this the elegant grown-up way with bowls of ice cream and a plate of the biscuits; or, my weakness, made up into sandwiches, the nubbly discs clasped round the soft, cold cream.

Two requests: don't use jumbo peanuts and don't use all butter. You need that Trex: quite apart from its trailer-trash charm, it's what makes them light.

75g light muscovado sugar, plus more for dipping later
100g unsalted butter
50g vegetable shortening such as Trex
1 large egg
1 teaspoon vanilla extract
175g self-raising flour
125g salted peanuts
2 baking sheets, lined

Preheat the oven to 190°C/gas mark 5.

In a large bowl, mix together the sugar, butter, shortening, egg and vanilla. Just beat it together, no ceremony, to combine well. You may find this easiest to do with an electric mixer. Stir in the flour and then the peanuts – and that's your dough done. Now, drop the dough in rounded teaspoons about 5cm apart onto the prepared baking sheets. Oil the bottom of a glass, or brush with melted butter, and dip it into some more light muscovado sugar and then press gently on the biscuits to flatten them.

Bake for 8–10 minutes, by which time they should be cooked through (though remember that biscuits always continue to cook for a while out of the oven), then remove to a wire rack to cool.

Makes about 30.

RICCIARELLI

I love these beautiful, bone-white Sienese macaroons. They're like soft, chewy, almond lozenges. I know it sounds odd to say use 300g ready-ground almonds or 500g blanched almonds which you then grind yourself, but as with the Spanish macaroons, the drier ready-ground ones absorb more liquid, so you need less. However, these are definitely better when you grind the nuts yourself – and I'm not asking you to do it by hand, but in a food processor for God's sake – so if you can, get them whole and blanched.

You have to start these the day before you want to eat them – not because any drastic action is required, but just because you need to let them dry out before baking them.

2 large egg whites
pinch of salt
225g caster sugar
zest of 1 lemon
1/2 teaspoon vanilla extract

1 teaspoon almond essence
300g ready-ground almonds or 500g whole blanched almonds, ground
icing sugar for dusting
2 baking sheets, lined

Whisk the egg whites and salt until they're stiff and dry, then gradually whisk in the sugar until you reach a marshmallowy consistency. Now add the lemon zest, vanilla extract and almond essence along with the ground almonds; mix to quite a hard paste.

Shape into small diamonds, dusting icing sugar over your hands to help you form the lozenges if the mixture's a little sticky. Lay on the baking sheets and leave to dry out overnight or for equivalent hours.

Heat the oven to 140°C/gas mark 1 and cook the ricciarelli for about 30 minutes, by which time they should be pale and slightly cracked. When cool, dust with icing sugar and serve.

These keep well in an airtight container.

Makes about 34.

Lemon gems, Granny Boyd's biscuits (p204) and sweet and salty peanut biscuits (p55)

LEMON GEMS

My children call these fried-egg biscuits and if you look at the photo you'll see why. But that doesn't convey the desirably acid intensity of their lemoniness. Of course, they are also sweet, but if you use good lemon curd (or make your own), they won't be too sweet: you will get that necesssary contrast between sharp, shining jellied curd, and buttery, sugared dough surround.

125g Trex, or other vegetable
   shortening
125g unsalted butter, softened
75g caster sugar
1 large egg yolk
1 tablespoon lemon juice
zest of 1 lemon

¹/4 teaspoon salt
275g plain flour
50g ground almonds
25g cornflour
6–7 tablespoons lemon curd
2 baking sheets, lined

Preheat the oven to 180°C/gas mark 4.

In a large bowl, beat the Trex, butter and sugar together, then add the egg yolk, lemon juice, zest and salt. Gently fold in the flour in two goes, then the ground almonds and cornflour. Take care not to be too heavy-handed, as rigorous blending will make it very sticky. It veers towards that anyway, so when all's combined, put the dough in the fridge to chill for at least an hour.

Form into balls the size of cherry tomatoes and place the dough 2¹/₂ cm apart on your prepared baking sheets. Make an indentation with your thumb in each biscuit, and then cook for 20–25 minutes. They should appear golden and firm.

As soon as they come out of the oven, fill each biscuit with a scant ¹/₂ teaspoon of lemon curd. When they're all filled, transfer them to wire racks to cool.

Makes about 40.

SAVOURY BISCUITS

IRISH BLUE BISCUITS

You don't need to use Irish cheese – though Cashel Blue does go particularly well here – nor do you need to worry about getting blue cornmeal if it eludes you (though I did find mine at the supermarket): these biscuits are delicious enough made with 175g of flour and with any robust but crumbly, creamy cheese, blue or otherwise.

175g Cashel Blue cheese, crumbled
100g unsalted butter, softened
1 large egg yolk
125g plain flour
50g blue cornmeal

pinch of salt (depending on saltiness
of cheese)
1 beaten egg for glazing (optional)
2 baking sheets, lined

Preheat the oven to 200°C/gas mark 6.

Mix the cheese, butter and egg yolk together and then work in the flour, cornmeal and the salt if you're using, just enough to form a soft dough. Form the dough into a fat disc, wrap it in clingflim and put in the fridge for 30 minutes or so to rest before it's rolled out. Dust a surface with flour (and sprinkle a little blue cornmeal onto it if you'd like) and roll out your cheese pastry to a thickness of about half a centimetre. Cut into whatever shapes you like; I quite like them squarish, but half-moons might be good, given the ingredients. If you're going to eat these by themselves, brush with the egg glaze before putting in the oven; if they're to be served with cheese (and they do go so well with the Cashel Blue of which they're partly made) leave them matt.

Cook for 10–15 minutes, by which time they'll be crisp at the edges and puffy in the middle. Remove to a wire rack to cool.

Makes about 30.

HOT DISCS

Think of these as a cross between tortilla chips and mini-poppadoms, the sort of biscuits that are perfect for dipping into salsa, hoummos or guacamole. Leave the seasonings out (bar the salt) and you have nineteenth-century Mereworth biscuits, to be eaten with soft cheese or the creamiest, unsalted butter.

Irish blue biscuits

STRAWBERRY SHORTCAKES

I've long been fascinated by this American pudding, which isn't really a scone so much as a tender, buttery sponge with scone-like properties, split and crammed with strawberries. There's so much dispute, as there always is with traditional recipes, over the right method to make them, serve them, eat them: should they be individual-sized or one huge fat disc? should butter be spread on the tender cut sides while still warm, before the fruit and cream are dolloped on?

I don't intend to enter into the debate – don't feel qualified to anyway – but since I'm a great fan of the methodical-to-the-point-of-obsessive American food magazine *Cook's Illustrated*, I got guidance from its executive editor Pam Anderson's book, *The Perfect Recipe*. I sometimes veer away from it, by using crème fraîche instead of whipped cream, or by using single cream in place of half-and-half (which we don't anyway have here) and I do like to sprinkle a little balsamic vinegar on the crushed strawberries, but in all respects that matter, this is her recipe.

This is what you want to bring out to people by the plateful on a summer's day after lunch in the garden.

for the shortcakes:

325g plain flour

1/2 teaspoon salt

1 tablespoon baking powder

5 tablespoons caster sugar

125g unsalted butter, frozen

1 large egg, beaten

125ml single cream

1 large egg white, lightly beaten

1 baking tray, greased or lined
61/2cm round cutter

for the filling:

approximately 300g strawberries

1 tablespoon caster sugar

few drops balsamic vinegar (optional)

250ml double cream or crème fraîche

Preheat the oven to 220°C/gas mark 7.

Mix the flour, salt, baking powder and 3 tablespoons of the sugar in a bowl. Grate the butter into these dry ingredients and use your fingertips to finish crumbling the butter into the flour. Whisk the egg into the cream, and pour into the flour mixture a little at a time, using a fork to mix. You may not need all of the eggy cream to make the dough come together, so go cautiously.

Turn the dough out onto a lightly floured surface, and roll gently to a thickness of about 2cm. Dip the cutter in flour and cut out as many rounds as you can. Work the scraps back into a dough, re-roll and finish cutting out – you should get 8 in all. Place the shortcakes about 2½cm apart on the baking sheet, brush the tops with the egg white, and sprinkle them with the remaining 2 tablespoons of caster sugar. If it helps with the rest of your cooking, or life in general, you can cover and refrigerate them now for up to 2 hours.

Bake for 10–15 minutes, until golden-brown, and let them cool for a short while on a wire rack. Meanwhile, crush half the strawberries with the spoonful of sugar and the few drops of balsamic vinegar if using, and halve or quarter the remaining straw-berries, depending on their size. Whip the double cream, if you're using.

The shortcakes should be eaten while still warm, so split each one across the middle and cover with a spoonful of the crushed strawberry mixture, a few halved or quartered strawberries, then dollop some whipped cream or crème fraîche on top, and set the top back on.

Makes 8.

VARIATION

I love these American-style with passionfruit in place of the strawberries, though if you're going along with this, don't use crème fraîche; you need velvety-smooth, whipped double cream, unpasteurized if possible.

Lily's scones (p67)

AMERICAN BREAKFAST PANCAKES

These are those thick, spongy American pancakes that are often eaten with warm maple syrup and crisp fried bacon. I love them with the syrup alone, but if you do want bacon, I think streaky is best: you want a crisp salty ribbon of it here. You can easily cook these pancakes by dolloping the batter onto a hot griddle (smooth, not ridged, side) or cast-iron pan, but I use a blini pan, one of my pet implements.

225g plain flour	**2 large eggs, beaten**
1 tablespoon baking powder	**30g butter, melted and cooled**
pinch of salt	**300ml milk**
1 teaspoon sugar	**butter for frying**

The easiest way to make these is to put all the ingredients into a blender and blitz. But if you do mix up the batter by hand in a bowl, make a well in the flour, baking powder, salt and sugar, beat in the eggs, melted butter and milk, and transfer to a jug: it's much easier to pour the batter into the pan than to spoon it. I like to leave the batter for 20 minutes before using it; and you may then want to add more milk to the mixture if you're frying in the blini pan, so that it runs right to the edges.

When you cook the pancakes, all you need to remember is that when the upper side of the pancake is blistering and bubbling it's time to cook the second side, and this needs only about 1 minute, if that.

I get 11 blini-pan-sized pancakes out of this, maybe 16 silver-dollar-sized ones on the griddle.

VARIATION
Sprinkle blueberries onto the uncooked side of the pancake just after you've poured the batter into the pan.

PIES

PIES

A pie is just what we all know should be emanating from the kitchen of a domestic goddess. Not simply because it is the traditional fare of the kitchen *Koenigin*, but because few things approach it when it comes to inducing that warm, bolstering sense of honourable satisfaction.

The truth is, however, that the less familiar pastry-making becomes, the harder we believe it to be; but all you have to do is make some and then you'll realize that it doesn't require expertise or dexterity beyond your capabilities. And I write as someone who is a clumsy and impatient cook. There is nothing like becoming competent at some hitherto terrifying activity to make one confident. And in cooking, as in everything else, confidence (and competence) breeds confidence. To learn how to make pastry, all I did was make some, and make it again. Then, some time later, again. Suddenly, I found I could do it, more or less without thinking about it. I'd never before considered myself a baker, and so it was particularly satisfying to become this person who turned out pastry and made pies and beautiful tarts.

But like the first kiss, it's the first pie that counts: as soon as I'd whipped it out of the oven and sprinkled sugar over it, I felt suffused with heady satisfaction. This was a real pie: the sort that I thought only women with sensible hands habitually wiped briskly on aprons could make. It changed my culinary self-image instantly. And that's why I am so evangelical now.

Perhaps the greatest joy of pastry-making is that it's mud-pie time; you get floury, sticky, wholly involved. I don't mean by this that you shouldn't use any equipment: I use my free-standing mixer, or processor.

(I need to, indeed, because I nearly always freeze the butter and flour together before combining as this helps you get a more feathery, flaky pastry.) But you still need to use your hands for that last crucial combining, the rolling, and draping into the tin, and the piecing-together of your pie.

Just do it.

Blackberry and apple pie (p118)

BASIC SHORTCRUST

The basic rule for pastry is that you use half the weight of fat to flour (and I nearly always prefer to make up that fat with equal amounts of butter and shortening and use 00 flour) and use a liquid – egg yolk, orange juice, whatever – to bind it. Throughout this chapter, though, and wherever necessary, I give precise ingredients for the particular recipe, so I give just my method here. What's more, it's foolproof; I was once that fool.

Put the flour in a shallow bowl, add the cold, diced fats and stir gently to coat. Put in the deep freeze – no need to cover – for 10 minutes. As you do so, put your liquid in a bowl or cup with a pinch of salt and transfer to the fridge. Either in a processor or – for choice – in a freestanding mixer with flat paddle, blend the fats and flour until you have a mixture that resembles sandy porridge. Then, gradually process or paddle in the liquid until the pastry is almost coming together. Use your hands now to form it into a disc or couple of discs, wrap in clingfilm and let it rest in the fridge for 20 minutes before rolling out.

PROCESSOR PUFF-PASTRY

Having discovered the world's most wonderful and hysterically easy Danish pastry (see p327), it occurred to me that the principle would surely apply to the un-yeasted version, that is to say, puff pastry. I tried it: it worked.

250g strong white flour
pinch of salt
250g cold unsalted butter, cut into
  1/2 cm slices

squeeze of lemon juice
5–6 tablespoons iced water

Pulse the flour and salt together in the processor, then add the cold butter and pulse 3–4 times; the pieces of butter should still be visible. Turn out into a large bowl and add a squeeze of lemon juice and enough iced water to bind the pastry. Wrap in clingfilm and rest in the fridge for half an hour.

Dust a surface with flour, roll the pastry out into a long rectangle, and fold in three like a business letter. Now turn the folded pastry so that if it was a book the spine would be on your left. Repeat twice more, turning every time.

Wrap again and rest in the fridge for another half-hour before you use it.

This makes enough for 2 x 20–25cm pie bases.

SAVOURY PIES

SUPPER ONION PIE

This is just what I want to eat for supper when it's dark early and I'm tired. It is a pie, yes, but not one with pastry that needs rolling out: you just make a cheese-scone dough and then press it over some onions, already softened and aromatic, in the pan.

for the filling/topping:
4 medium red onions (about 750g)
1 tablespoon olive oil
1 heaped tablespoon butter (about 25g)
3–4 sprigs of thyme, de-stalked, or ½ teaspoon dried thyme
150g strong Cheddar cheese or Gruyère, grated

for the scone dough:
250g plain flour
1 scant teaspoon baking powder
1 teaspoon salt
100ml milk
40g butter, melted
1 scant teaspoon English mustard
1 large egg, beaten
20–25cm cast-iron skillet or 24cm pie dish, buttered

Preheat the oven to 200°C/gas mark 6. Peel the onions, halve them, then cut each half into 4 segments each. Heat the oil and butter in the pan, then add the onions and cook over a medium heat, stirring regularly, for about 30 minutes; they should be soft and tinged with colour. Season with salt and pepper, and add the thyme. Turn into a pie dish, and scatter 50g of the cheese over the waiting onions. Leave while you get on with the dough topping.

Put the flour, baking powder and salt together in a bowl with the remaining cheese. Pour the milk into a measuring jug, add the melted butter, mustard and egg, mix well and then pour onto the flour mixture in the bowl. Mix to a dough using a fork, a wooden spoon or your hands; it should be quite sticky. Then tip it out onto a work surface and press into a circle about the size of the pie dish. Transfer it to the dish, pressing it to seal the edges.

Put it in the oven for 15 minutes, then turn down to 180°C/gas mark 4 and give it another 10 minutes, by which time the dough should be golden and crisp on top. Let it stand for a couple of minutes, then cover with a large plate and turn upside-down so the plate's beneath and the pie dish on top. Place on a flat surface and remove the dish.

I love this with brown sauce, either home-made (see the domestic goddess's larder, p362) or bought HP.

Makes 6 generous slices.

PIZZA RUSTICA

Pizza rustica is not a pizza in the way that we've come to understand it, though anyone who's spent time in Italy might well have come across it. The word pizza simply means pie, and this term denotes a deep, pastry-encased creation, stuffed with relatively unfancy ingredients. For a non-Italian, however, these ingredients are at the upper end of the economic scale, and hardly rustica at all, and it's for this reason I thought up my pizza rustica *all'inglese* (see below), though any Italian deli should be able to supply you with the wherewithal easily enough, and increasingly the supermarkets stock what you'll need too. The wonderful Anna del Conte gave me this recipe – from her magnum opus, *The Gastronomy of Italy*. Using a Springform tin rather than pie dish makes the building-up of the pie easy, and the finished, unmoulded creation looks a miracle of proud, golden accomplishment.

for the pastry:
250g plain flour, preferably Italian 00
125g cold unsalted butter, cut into 1cm cubes
2 egg yolks
2 tablespoons iced water
1 heaped teaspoon salt
1 tablespoon caster sugar
22cm Springform tin, buttered

for the filling:
50g luganega or mild pure pork sausage, skinned
1 tablespoon olive oil
250g ricotta
50g smoked provolone, diced
125g Italian mozzarella, crumbled

50g freshly grated parmesan
1/2 clove garlic, chopped
2 tablespoons chopped flat-leaf parsley
2 pinches chilli powder or crushed dried red chillies
100g prosciutto, cut into small pieces
100g mortadella, cut into small pieces
2 eggs, lightly beaten
black pepper
1 heaped tablespoon dried breadcrumbs

for the glaze:
1 egg yolk
2 tablespoons milk
pinch of salt

Put the flour and butter in a dish, and put this dish in the deep freeze for 10 minutes. Stir together the yolks, water and salt in a cup, and put this cup in the fridge. Then, when time's up, tip the flour and butter into the bowl of the processor, add the sugar and pulse to combine: you want a soft crumbly mass, somewhere between sand and porridge oats. Bind with the egg yolks, water and salt, and when it looks like it's on the verge of coming together (you have to stop slightly short of this actually happening), tip the pastry out and wedge it together with your hands. Don't worry, though, if the pastry is

COURGETTE AND CHICK PEA FILO PIE

We're still in the realm of the Springform here, but it is, nevertheless, a different sort of pie. Quite simply, it's a pie for those of you who don't want to make pastry. I know that you can buy shortcrust not only ready-made but ready-rolled, but that never seems a happy choice to me; buying ready-made filo pastry, on the other hand, is quite simply what you do. (Though, until recently, I was far more frightened of taking the filo sheets from the box than I was of making my own basic pastry.) Correspondingly, I use tinned chick peas, though please feel free to soak and cook the dried ones if you prefer.

I can't claim this as an Iranian creation, but I certainly had the tastes and fragrances of some Iranian dishes in mind.

¹/₂ teaspoon cumin seeds

1 small onion or ¹/₂ a large onion, finely diced

2 tablespoons olive oil

¹/₂ teaspoon turmeric

1 teaspoon ground coriander

3 plump courgettes

125g basmati rice

500ml vegetable stock, or chicken if you prefer

2 x 425g can of chick peas, drained

100g melted butter

200g filo pastry

22cm Springform tin

Preheat the oven to 200°C/gas mark 6 and put in a baking sheet.

Gently fry the cumin seeds and onion in the olive oil until the onion's soft. Add the turmeric and coriander. Dice the courgettes (unpeeled), add them to the onion mixture, and cook on a fairly high heat to prevent the courgettes becoming watery. When they are soft but still holding their shape, add the rice and stir well, letting the rice become well coated in the oil. Add the stock 100ml at a time, stirring while you do so. When all the liquid has been absorbed the rice should be cooked, so take it off the heat, stir in the chick peas and check the seasoning.

Brush the insides of the Springform tin with some of the melted butter. Line the bottom and sides of the tin with ³/₄ of the filo, buttering each piece as you layer. Leave a little filo overlapping the sides, and keep 3–4 layers for the top. Carefully put in your slightly cooled filling, and then fold in the overlaps. Butter the last layers of filo and scrunch on top of the pie as a covering. Brush with a final coat of butter, and put in the oven for about 20 minutes, or until the filo is golden and the middle hot. Check this by inserting a slim, sharp-bladed knife (or cake-tester). If, when you remove it, it feels hot when you press it against your wrist, the pie's ready.

Serves 6–8.

STEAK AND KIDNEY PUDDING

You may think that a steak and kidney pudding made with a thick suet crust is not the sort of food you eat. All I can say is cook it and you'll change your mind. When we made this for the photographic shoot, we, to a woman, wolfed it down with what I can only describe as besotted greed.

Contrary to most people's preconceptions, suet gives the crust an almost ethereal lightness. True, this is only the case if it's eaten immediately – any standing around and it seems to seize up and gain thick-set density – but eat fast and it'll still be delicious when you get round to second helpings. I always use vegetable suet, as I don't like eating meat products whose derivation I do not know. The only thing I'd add is that while suet crust is very easy to make, you must make it at the last minute.

As for equipment: life is very much easier if you buy a plastic pudding basin with a fitted lid than if you use a traditional basin and make a pleated foil lid and string handles. You don't need to steam the pudding: you can simply immerse it in a large pan of boiling water.

I often double the quantities for the meat filling, then freeze half, so I'm only a defrost away from another pudding. Traditionally, oysters were added to steak and kidney pud; I thought a little oyster sauce might be an appropriate contemporary adaptation, and it was, rewardingly so. And I happened to find some beer called Oyster Stout which seemed entirely right for it too, but it's hardly essential: any stout in a storm . . .

I always cook the meat filling a day or two in advance: the flavours deepen wonderfully and the whole thing seems less of a performance.

for the filling:

2 tablespoons flour
1/2 teaspoon English mustard powder
500g stewing steak, cut into 2cm
   pieces
250g lambs' kidney, cut into chunks
25g butter
2 tablespoons olive oil
1 medium onion, chopped
150g flat mushrooms (i.e., 2 medium-
   sized), peeled and roughly chunked

150ml beef stock
150ml stout
1 scant tablespoon oyster sauce

for the suet crust:

350g self-raising flour
1/2 teaspoon salt
175g suet
1/2 teaspoon English mustard powder
3-litre plastic pudding basin with lid,
   both well buttered

The 2 hours of steaming – which involves little activity on your part – seems less of a consideration when separated from the pudding's preparation. So, preheat the oven to 140°C/gas mark 1, season the 2 tablespoons of flour with salt, pepper and the mustard

CHEESE, ONION AND POTATO PIES

This is the picnic food of fondest imagination, although actually we eat these for ordinary tea in the kitchen fairly often. I say 'we': that's to say I make them for the children, then snaffle down a couple myself. I love them as much cold as warm, which is why I've suggested you make eight.

The trick, if trick it be, is to use spring onions, which have all the flavour but none of the BO-ey breath of the usual onion, as in cheese & onion, component.

I use Yorkshire pudding tins, with their wide, shallow indentations, for these, and prefer that more English, even rustic, look. But if you wanted to use individual flan tins, of course you could.

for the pastry:
2 large egg yolks
1 heaped teaspoon salt
2 tablespoons cold water
250g flour
35g Trex or other vegetable shortening, teaspooned out
90g cold unsalted butter, diced
2 x 4-bun Yorkshire pudding trays

for the filling:
500g potatoes (waxy not floury)
100g spring onions (about 6) chopped finely
125g mature Cheddar: 75g grated, 50g diced
2 tablespoons grated parmesan
50g Red Leicester, grated
2 tablespoons chopped parsley
4 tablespoons crème fraîche to bind

Make the pastry by the usual method (see p83), then halve it, form each half into a disc, wrap in clingfilm and leave in the fridge for 20 minutes.

Preheat the oven to 200°C/gas mark 6.

Meanwhile, peel and dice the potatoes, put them in a saucepan with plenty of cold water and bring to the boil. Boil gently for 5–10 minutes, or until the cubes are cooked but still retain their shape. Drain and leave to cool.

In a large bowl, combine the spring onions, cheeses, slightly cooled potato and parsley. Bind with the crème fraîche and season with salt and pepper. Roll out one of the pastry discs, cut 8 rough circles slightly larger than the indents and push 4 into the first tray to make the bases. Fill each with an eighth of the mixture and put the remaining 4 circles on as lids. Seal the pie edges with the back of a knife, making a little hole in each one. Repeat for the second tray with the other disc and the remaining half of the filling.

Cook for 20 minutes, by which time the pastry should be firm, beginning to turn gold, but still pale, and let the pies stand a little out of the oven in their trays before easing them out of the moulds.

Makes 8.

SMALL TOMATO TARTS

These, which are so much lighter and fresher than you could ever hope for, are just what I want for lunch when it's warm enough to eat outside, but they'd make an equally good starter for a dinner party. I make the pastry with cornmeal for crispness and to prevent sogginess, but this kind of pastry is quite friable, so I wouldn't want to make a larger tart to cut into wedges – hence my willingness to live with the individual portions. But old prejudices die hard: I'd arrange them all on one large oval dish for people to help themselves rather than plate them up singly in advance.

for the pastry:
125g flour, preferably Italian 00
60g fine cornmeal or polenta
1 tablespoon caster sugar
1/2 teaspoon salt
115g butter
25g Trex or other vegetable shortening
40–50ml iced water, or enough to bind
8 individual tart tins (12cm x 2cm)

for the filling:
495–500g tin chopped tomatoes
pinch sugar
50g pecorino cheese sliced into thin slivers with a potato peeler
15g packet or small handful basil, finely shredded
32 (approximately 500g) baby tomatoes, halved around the equator
32 black olives in oil, halved

First make the pastry: pulse the dry ingredients in the processor, then add the butter and shortening, diced into small pieces. Pulse briefly until the mixture resembles coarse breadcrumbs, then add enough iced water to form a dough, pulsing with the gentlest touch to combine. Form into two discs, wrap with clingfilm and refrigerate for 30 minutes.

Roll out one of the pastry discs into a rough square. Cut into 4 squares (each piece should be big enough to fill the small tart case) and drape into the tins, folding the edges inward. Repeat with the other disc of pastry and the 4 remaining tins, and put them back in the fridge for 15 minutes. Preheat the oven to 200°C/gas mark 6, putting in a couple of baking sheets as you do so.

Meanwhile, empty the tinned tomatoes into a bowl, and season well with salt, pepper and a pinch of sugar. To arrange the tarts, put a thin layer of tomato mix, then 3 slices of pecorino cheese on top, then a sprinkling of basil, then 8 tomato halves with 8 olive halves in rows, and finally a grind of pepper.

Cook for 20 minutes on the baking sheets and let the tarts stand a bit, on a rack out of the oven, before you take them out of their tins.

Makes 8.

RHUBARB TART

This is perfect for January, when the new season's forced rhubarb is just in, rosy and budding with its rhubarbiness. (Actually, Marks & Spencer sells exquisite stuff for a few months more.) It's made all the more dazzling by the contrast with the snowy whiteness of the filling beneath. And I like the neatness of this, in shopping terms at least: you need the cream cheese for the pastry, so why not use it as well for the smooth and voluptuous interior? I know it looks as if there's a lot of fat per flour for the pastry, but go with it.

for the filling:
1kg rhubarb (untrimmed weight)
300g caster sugar

for the pastry:
150g plain flour
1 tablespoon caster sugar
1/4 teaspoon salt
85g cold unsalted butter, diced
85g cold cream cheese, diced
2–3 tablespoons cold double cream to bind

1 deep 23cm flan tin or shallow 25cm tin

for the cream-cheese filling:
200g cream cheese
200ml double cream
2 tablespoons caster sugar
4 tablespoons muscat or rum

for the glaze:
6 tablespoons rhubarb juice, reserved from stewing

Heat the oven to 190°C/gas mark 5.

Trim and cut the rhubarb into 2cm pieces, place in a shallow ovenproof dish (I use a Pyrex dish of about 20cm x 30cm), pour the sugar over the rhubarb and toss it all together so the sugar's well dispersed. Cover with foil and cook for about 45 minutes, or until tender. When you take the rhubarb out, slip in a baking sheet. When the rhubarb's cool, strain it and reserve the juice.

Meanwhile, get on with making the pastry. Using a food processor, mix the dry ingredients, then add the butter and cheese and pulse to make a crumbly mixture. Bind with the cream, pulsing sparingly. Let the pastry rest in the fridge for at least 20 minutes before lining your tart tin. After you've rolled the pastry out and lined the tin with it, put it back in the fridge for another 20 minutes.

Remove from the fridge and line with foil. Fill the pastry case with baking beans (though you could just as well use any dried beans) and put on the sheet in the oven for 15 minutes. Gingerly remove the beans and foil – bearing in mind their heat – and cook for a further 5 minutes or until it's turning golden-brown and is cooked through. Leave to cool on a wire rack.

BLACK AND WHITE TART

I apologize for the slightly eighties ring to the title, but I can't help myself. You could use any berries here, but I made this to wallow in the sheer beauty of the blackberries and whitecurrants of the last summer of the last century. And before you start mewing to yourself about the difficulties of unearthing such rare treasures, I should tell you that Sainsbury's regularly stocks them in season. This is one of the easiest tarts you could make: a cheesecake base, the filling a mascarpone cream, and the berries dropped like gleaming gems – jet and moonstone – on top.

for the base:

250g digestives, roughly broken

75g unsalted butter, melted

25cm fluted flan tin, 3½cm deep

for the filling and topping:

1 large egg, separated

75g caster sugar

500g mascarpone

squeeze of lime or lemon (to taste)

1 tablespoon tequila or white rum, optional

400g blackberries

100g whitecurrants

Put the biscuits in the processor and blitz to crumbs. Then, motor running, add the melted butter down the funnel. Tip into the flan case and, using your fingers, press onto the base and up the sides. Put in the fridge while you get on with the creamy filling-cum-topping.

Whisk the egg white until stiff but not dry and set aside for a moment. Beat the yolk with the sugar until thick and pale; you may think there's too much sugar to make a paste, but persist: it happens. Add the mascarpone, beating till smooth, then the lime or lemon juice and the rum, if using. Fold in the egg white and pile and smooth this mixture into the prepared flan case. Arrange the blackberries and whitecurrants on top, but loosely. You should, for ease of eating, remove most of the stalks and stems, but I like to leave some still on for beauty's sake.

Serves 8.

VARIATION

You can alter the fruit as you like, and certainly don't feel constrained to stick with berries. The best and freshest peaches are wonderful, as are figs, and in winter you could soak and cook dried figs or apricots, arrange the fruit on the cream, then drizzle over some reduced cooking liquid.

BLACKBERRY GALETTE

This is really a free-form pizza-like tart, which I made for the first time while we were doing the photography for this book. We happened to have some polenta pastry left over and some spare blackberries in the fridge and I, suddenly rebelling against the planning and rule-following necessary to get all the food photographed, played around. This was the result. And really, you could use any fruit. I'd stick with the polenta or cornmeal pastry only because nothing soaks up the fruit's juices better without going soggy.

for the pastry:
60g plain flour
30g polenta/fine cornmeal
1 scant tablespoon caster sugar
¹/₄ teaspoon salt
50g cold butter
15g (1 tablespoon) vegetable shortening
1–3 tablespoons iced water or enough to bind

1 baking sheet, lined

for the filling:
1 punnet blackberries (approximately 150g)
approximately 3 tablespoons caster sugar
3 heaped tablespoons crème fraîche, plus more to serve

In a food processor, pulse the dry ingredients, then add the butter and shortening diced into small pieces. Pulse briefly until it resembles coarse breadcrumbs, then add enough iced water to form a dough, pulsing gently to mix. Form it into a disc, wrap in clingfilm and put in the fridge to rest for about 30 minutes.

Preheat the oven to 190°C/gas mark 5. Roll the pastry out into a rough circle, transfer to the baking sheet and scatter blackberries on top, leaving a good 7cm margin round the edge. Sprinkle with 1–2 tablespoons sugar, to taste, then dollop with crème fraîche. Sprinkle a further tablespoonful of sugar over, dampen the edges with water, then wrap them over themselves to form a knobbly, ramshackle rim and put in the oven for about 20 minutes or until the pastry is cooked through.

Serves 6.

DOUBLE APPLE PIE

I don't want to nominate favourites, but even so, I have to say this is a pie I am ecstatic about – perhaps because it's so far removed from what I've spent my life cooking.

The notion of putting Cheddar in the pastry of an apple pie is not a new one but I was pleased all the same to see how well it worked. I've used a Springform tin (learning a lesson from the pizza rustica, above), which makes this a good, hefty, sliceable pie.

The double-apple element – Coxes to hold their shape, Bramleys to make for an appley-velvet background – does entail quite a bit of work, but it isn't difficult work, just moderately time-consuming. Anyone who's hanging about the house claiming to want to help should be handed a vegetable peeler and an apple corer without delay.

for the pastry:
50g cold unsalted butter, diced
50g Trex or other vegetable
 shortening
250g self-raising flour
50g finely grated Cheddar
1 large egg
iced water to bind
pinch of salt
22cm Springform tin

for the filling:
750g Bramley apples (about 3 large),
 peeled and cored
1kg Cox apples (about 10), peeled,
 cored and cut into eighths
80g unsalted butter
pinch of ground cloves
good grating of nutmeg
2 large eggs, beaten
100g caster sugar

Make the pastry in a food processor as normal: pulse the butter and Trex into the flour until it looks like crumbs. Leaving the mixture in the bowl, put the grating blade in and process the cheese into the crumb mixture. Replace the normal blade, and add the egg, iced water and salt to bind. Turn the pastry out and press it into two discs, one slightly smaller than the other. Wrap each in clingfilm and put them in the fridge to rest for at least 20 minutes.

Preheat the oven to 200°C/gas mark 6, putting in a baking sheet. Slice the Bramleys into small chunks and fry in half the butter until they become soft and begin to lose their shape. Add the cloves and nutmeg. Tip the apple mush into the food processor, and purée, pulsing so as not to make it too like baby food. Add about three-quarters of the beaten egg and all of the sugar and pulse again to mix. Fry the Coxes in the other half of the butter and cover them to help them cook a little. Cook for about 10 minutes: they should be tender but still holding their shape.

Roll out the larger disc of pastry and line the tin with it, letting it hang over the sides. Pour in the puréed mixture, and then push the Cox pieces into the purée to coat them. Roll out the smaller disc of pastry to form the top. Lay over the pie, and curl the

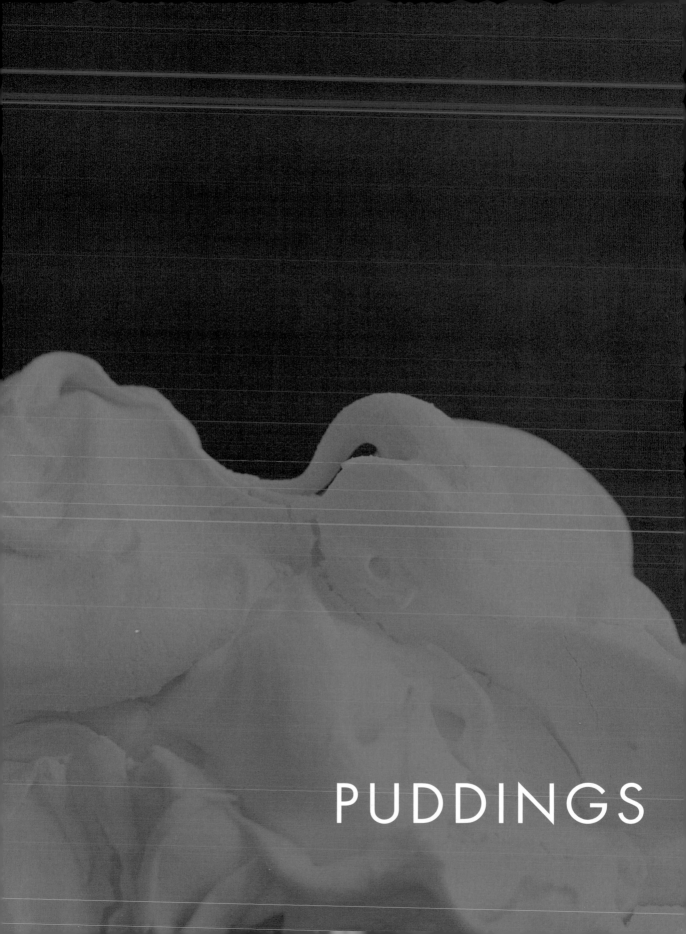

PUDDINGS

PUDDINGS

When I was a restaurant critic, I was once teased for talking about 'the pudding' and then proceeding to describe some elaborate, light and most definitely unpuddingy French confection. But pudding is the word I stick to: can't help it and don't want to. Regardless of style or substance, if it's intended for the last, sweet course, it's pudding in my book. That's not to say that several of the recipes elsewhere in this book couldn't also be made and served up as pudding; indeed, given that we no longer eat tea to any convincing degree, the chances are most of them will end up that way. (That's if you don't count the stand-up breakfast comprising wolfed-down leftovers stashed overnight in the fridge.)

On the whole, I take the line that you do not have to make pudding: the French have always bought their pâtisserie from those who really know how to do it. But in fact there is a good, lazy reason to cook pudding: unless you go out of your way to choose something complicated, the chances are that the process will not be difficult, and the reward gratifying. Quite apart from that essential sense of private satisfaction, people really do seem far more impressed by a home-made pudding, however simple, than they would be by the most lovingly produced main course. You know I'm not a cook-to-impress kind of a girl, so my point isn't so much that you can luxuriate in the astonished admiration of your friends by cooking pudding, but you can thereby lessen the culinary load all round.

Do you know how easy it is to make a steamed sponge? You just bung all the ingredients in a processor, blitz and scrape into a pudding bowl and then sit the pudding bowl in boiling water for a couple of hours. In that time, you are required to do nothing, except maybe for the odd topping-up from the kettle so the pan doesn't boil dry. In other words, this is the easy option, the comforting one – for cook and cookee. What more do you want?

STEAMED SYRUP SPONGE

Even though this pudding takes 2 hours to cook, that isn't as awkward as it sounds. You can assemble it all very quickly, and if you're serving it for a dinner party on a working day, just get started the minute you get in, before you've even taken your coat off, and then you should have no problems about timing.

Not being particularly good with my hands, I don't go in for all that foil-pleating farrago: I just use a plastic pudding basin which is manufactured for the purpose and comes with its own lid which fits. (Don't put either bowl or lid in the dishwasher, however, or the next time you use it it won't.)

I cannot tell you how glorious this is: light beyond words, feathery textured and comfortingly, not cloyingly, sweet. I know steamed sponges are so out of favour as to be, generally, beyond consideration now, but please do yourself a favour: cook it, eat it and then tell me . . .

for the sponge:
**175g very soft unsalted butter, plus
more for greasing**
175g self-raising flour
175g caster sugar
3 large eggs
**zest of 1 unwaxed lemon and juice
of 1/2**

3 tablespoons milk

for the syrup base/topping:
250g golden syrup
juice of other 1/2 lemon
1 3/4 litre pudding basin with lid

Put the kettle on, then put the butter, flour, sugar, eggs, lemon and milk in the food processor and whizz together, adding a little more milk if the mix is too thick (it should be a thick, pouring consistency).

Pour the boiling water into a large saucepan which has a lid (the water should come about half to two-thirds of the way up the side of the pudding basin when in) or into the base of a steamer. Put it on the heat. Meanwhile, butter the pudding basin, put the golden syrup in the bottom of it and stir in the lemon juice. Pour the sponge mixture on top of the syrup and put on the plastic lid, remembering to butter it first. Then put the pudding basin into the saucepan, put the lid on the saucepan, and that's it. The pan should keep just boiling, with the lid on. The important thing is that it shouldn't boil dry. Keep some water hot in the kettle to pour in when necessary.

I know one is supposed to put the basin on a saucer in the pan, but the rattling noise it makes drives me mad, and the pudding doesn't seem to suffer for being un-triveted. Let it cook for a minimum of 2 hours, more won't matter. When it's ready, remove (I don't bother to make a handle out of string, but use two spatulas to lift it out

OM ALI

I first ate this at Ali Baba, an Egyptian restaurant in London to which I was taken by Claudia Roden, about 10 years ago. How I remembered it, when I came to cook it myself, was as a kind of Egyptian bread-and-butter pudding; certainly, the idea is the same. Filo pastry is buttered and baked, then layered with nuts and dried fruit in a dish into which you pour cream-enriched sweetened milk before baking it again.

It looks beautiful – the white, the gold, the amber, the green – and it tastes just how you might imagine it would: light, comforting, fragrant. And, like most of the puddings here, it's extremely easy to make. I cook it in a dish made by Calphalon called an Everyday Pan, mainly because it's graceful, unfancy and it looks the part, but any normal-sized (approximately 20cm) pie dish should be fine.

200g filo pastry
100g butter, melted, plus some for greasing
60g sultanas
75g dried apricots, diced small
75g flaked almonds
50g pistachios, chopped

50g pine nuts
1 litre full fat milk
300ml double cream
100g caster sugar
fresh nutmeg
2 baking sheets
20cm pie dish

Preheat the oven to 150°C/gas mark 2

Paint the filo sheets with melted butter and crumple loosely like wet rags, dividing them between the baking sheets. Cook for about 20 minutes until they turn crispy and golden.

Now turn your oven up to 240°C/gas mark 9. Butter the dish you're using and crumble the filo pastry into it to cover the bottom, then sprinkle the sultanas, apricots and nuts on top, and continue layer by layer until all is used up. Heat the milk, cream and sugar in a saucepan, and bring to the boil. As soon as it's come to the boil, pour over the filo and fruit layers, grate over some fresh nutmeg and then put the dish back into the oven for 10–15 minutes. The top should be lightly browned, burnished and billowed up with the heat. Leave for a few minutes before spooning into small bowls.

Serves 6–8.

PISTACHIO SOUFFLÉS

Normally I hate the individually portioned, the mealy-mouthed ramekin of professional practice. But I make exceptions. I've made pistachio soufflé in one large dish and loved it, but you just don't get that perfect ratio of heat-singed exterior and tender interior unless you use dishes with a small diameter.

I have a particular love for pistachios, their scent, their fragrant, delicate taste, that clean eau-de-nil colour, those romantic, *Arabian Nights* associations. The square of dark chocolate, hidden dark and melting within, is the soufflés' killer secret. Don't ruin it by announcing it beforehand.

Lindt Excellence is a good chocolate to use here, because it comes in bars already scored with squares exactly the right size to be pressed into a ramekin (and it's generally stocked by supermarkets and sweet shops). This picture was taken in a huge, cold studio in the dead of winter. I promise you that they rose higher, as yours will too.

30g soft unsalted butter, plus extra for greasing soufflé cups

60g caster sugar, plus extra for dusting soufflé cups, plus 1 tablespoon for the egg whites

20g plain flour

150ml full-fat milk

4 large eggs separated

100g pistachios (peeled weight), ground

2 drops almond extract

1/2 teaspoon vanilla extract

1/2 teaspoon orange-flower water

5 large egg whites

pinch of salt

6 x 10g squares, or similar, good dark chocolate

icing sugar for dusting over

6 x 250ml ramekins or soufflé dishes

Preheat the oven to 200°C/gas mark 6 and put in a baking sheet. Use a little butter to grease the insides of the ramekins and then tip in a little caster sugar, swirl about to cover, and tip out the excess.

Put the flour in a saucepan and add a little milk, just to blend. Then, stirring (I tend to use one of those little Magiwhisks here, but a wooden spoon would do fine as long as you're patient), add the rest of the milk and 60g sugar. Whisk over a medium heat until it comes to boiling point, then whisk for 30 seconds and take off the heat, by which time it should be very thick. Let it cool a little, then add the yolks, whisking in one at a time.

If you're making this in advance, beat in half of the butter and dot the rest on the top to stop a skin forming; otherwise just beat in all the butter now.

Add the ground pistachios, the almond and vanilla extracts and the orange-flower water, and mix in well. Then, whisk all 5 egg whites together with the salt until

LONDON CHEESECAKE

If I had a New York cheesecake, I had to have a London one, and this is surely it. My paternal grandmother instructed me in the art of adding the final layer of sour cream, sugar and vanilla: and it's true, it does complete it.

I cannot tell you how much the velvety smoothness is enhanced by cooking the cheesecake in the water bath. It's not hard, though you really must wrap the tin twice in extra-strength tin foil. Once you've tried it this way, you won't even consider cooking it any other.

for the base:

150g digestive biscuits

75g unsalted butter, melted or very soft

600g cream cheese

150g caster sugar

3 large eggs

3 large egg yolks

1 1/2 tablespoons vanilla extract

1 1/2 tablespoons lemon juice

20cm Springform tin

extra-strength tin foil

for the topping:

145ml tub sour cream

1 tablespoon caster sugar

1/2 teaspoon vanilla extract

Process the biscuits until they are like crumbs, then add the butter and pulse again. Line the bottom of the Springform tin, pressing the biscuits in with your hands or the back of a spoon. Put the tin in the fridge to set, and preheat the oven to 180°C/gas mark 4.

Beat the cream cheese gently until it's smooth, then add the sugar. Beat in the eggs and egg yolks, then finally the vanilla and lemon juice. Put the kettle on.

Line the outside of the chilled tin with strong foil so that it covers the bottom and sides in one large piece, and then do the same again and put it into a roasting dish. This will protect the cheesecake from the water as it is cooked in its water bath.

Pour the cream-cheese filling into the chilled biscuit base, and then pour hot water from the recently boiled kettle into the roasting tin around the cheesecake. It should come about halfway up; don't overfill as it will be difficult to lift up the tin. Put it into the oven and cook for 50 minutes. It should feel set, but not rigidly so: you just need to feel confident that when you pour the sour cream over, it will sit on the surface and not sink in. Whisk together the sour cream, sugar and vanilla for the topping and pour over the cheesecake. Put it back in the oven for a further 10 minutes.

Take the roasting tin out of the oven, then gingerly remove the Springform, unwrap it and stand it on a rack to cool. When it's cooled down completely, put it in the fridge, removing it 20 minutes before eating to take the chill off. Unmould and when you cut into it, plunge a knife in hot water first.

Serves 8.

CHOCOLATE

CHOCOLATE

If you asked me, I'd say that, unlike a lot of people I know, I am not particularly keen on chocolate. So why did this chapter grow more quickly than all the other chapters in the book? Well, it turns out there really are times when only chocolate will do. But for me, chocolate has to be good, not just brown and sweet. Actually, I'd go further: chocolate, in cooking, is better the less sweet, the more subtle it is.

While I don't want to get tiresomely prescriptive, it's obvious that the chocolate you choose is crucial to the brownies or cakes you make. I have a preference for Montgomery Moore buttons – dark, milk or white (the only white chocolate I'd ever want to eat); the chocolate is extraordinarily, seductively good, and melts beautifully and quickly, but these buttons can be hard to come by. Luckily, Nestlé do chocolate buttons and lumps now too, which you may find more easily in the supermarket. Buying your chocolate already chopped saves time, but is hardly an imperative. Just stock up on the best bars of chocolate you can find, such as Valrhona, and proper, cooked-earth-coloured cocoa. Look for brands containing a minimum of 70 per cent cocoa solids. When in doubt, or in need, phone the Chocolate Society (01423 322 230).

One last thing: melting. The traditional method is to put broken-up pieces of chocolate in a bowl and that bowl on top of a pan of simmering water, making sure that the base of the bowl never comes into contact with the water (it is the steam that melts it). I am, however a complete convert to the microwave for this. I'm not quite enough of a microwave queen, though, to be confident of giving you precise instructions. What I do is give 100g of broken-up chocolate about a minute on medium, then look to see if another minute's required. Not only is it easier to melt chocolate in the microwave than in a bowl over a pan of water, but it's much harder, even in my clumsy experience, to burn it so that it seizes up and becomes expensively unusable. Though if this does happen to you, you might be able to save it by whisking in, off the heat, a knob of butter or drop of vegetable oil. But it's safer to use the microwave and proceed slowly – a hard proviso for the impatient cook, I know, but if I can do it, so can you.

DENSE CHOCOLATE LOAF CAKE

I start with this because I think it is the essence of all that is desirable in chocolate: its dark intensity isn't toyed with, nor upstaged by any culinary elaboration. This is the plainest of plain loaf cakes – but that doesn't convey the damp, heady aromatic denseness of it. To understand that, you just have to cook it. And as you'll see, that isn't hard at all.

I also think this makes a wonderful pudding, either by itself with ice cream or, as when my in-laws were round for lunch one Sunday, with a bowl of strawberries and a jug of white-chocolate rum custard. The latter is a fussier option, but there are times when that's, perversely, what we want.

But simply sliced, with a cup of tea or coffee, it's pretty damn dreamy: as damp and sticky as gingerbread and quite as aromatic. And I will confess that I absolutely love it spread with cold cream cheese.

225g soft unsalted butter
375g dark muscovado sugar
2 large eggs, beaten
1 teaspoon vanilla extract
100g best dark chocolate, melted

200g plain flour
1 teaspoon bicarbonate of soda
250ml boiling water
23 x 13 x 7cm loaf tin

Preheat the oven to 190°C/gas mark 5, put in a baking sheet in case of sticky drips later, and grease and line the loaf tin. The lining is important as this is a very damp cake: use parchment, Bake-O-Glide or one of those loaf-tin-shaped paper cases.

Cream the butter and sugar, either with a wooden spoon or with an electric hand-held mixer, then add the eggs and vanilla, beating in well. Next, fold in the melted and now slightly cooled chocolate, taking care to blend well but being careful not to overbeat. You want the ingredients combined: you don't want a light airy mass. Then gently add the flour, to which you've added the bicarb, alternately spoon by spoon, with the boiling water until you have a smooth and fairly liquid batter. Pour into the lined loaf tin, and bake for 30 minutes. Turn the oven down to 170°C/gas mark 3 and continue to cook for another 15 minutes. The cake will still be a bit squidgy inside, so an inserted cake-tester or skewer won't come out completely clean.

Place the loaf tin on a rack, and leave to get completely cold before turning it out. (I often leave it for a day or so: like gingerbread, it improves.) Don't worry if it sinks in the middle: indeed, it will do so because it's such a dense and damp cake.

Makes 8–10 slices.

WHITE-CHOCOLATE RUM CUSTARD

And here's one way of transforming your cake into the perfect Sunday-lunch pudding. Simply follow the instructions for the custard on p134, omitting the vanilla, using only a scant tablespoonful of sugar and adding 1–2 tablespoons of dark rum. Then, when the custard's thick, beat in 100g of melted white chocolate off the heat. Leave to cool in a jug or bowl, but remember to cover the top with a piece of damp baking parchment to prevent it forming a skin. Throw some halved, lightly sugared strawberries into a bowl to serve alongside if the idea appeals.

VARIATION

I sometimes make these aromatic chocolate cupcakes to take as a present if we're going away for the weekend: they look so wonderful studded with gold Smarties, though actually a plain, shiny-brown Minstrel would have a certain chic allure.

for the cakes:

110g unsalted butter

200g dark muscovado sugar

1 large egg, beaten

½ teaspoon vanilla extract

**50g dark chocolate, melted and
  cooled a little**

100g plain flour

½ teaspoon bicarbonate soda

125ml boiling water

12-bun muffin tin with paper cases

for the icing:

175g dark chocolate

75g milk chocolate

200ml double cream

½ teaspoon vanilla extract

**12 gold Smarties, gold leaf or other
  decorations of your choice**

Preheat the oven to 180°C/gas mark 4.

Using the method above, make the batter and fill the 12 muffin paper cases in the muffin tin. Bake for 30 minutes, remove from the tin and cool on a rack.

To make the icing, break all the chocolate into pieces (if no children are eating these you may prefer to use all dark chocolate) and heat with the cream and vanilla in a saucepan until it has melted. Whisk until it's a good consistency for icing, and spoon some onto each thoroughly cooled cake. Spread with the back of the spoon and stud each one with a gold Smartie or decorate as you wish. Leave to set somewhere cool, though preferably not in the fridge.

SOUR-CREAM CHOCOLATE CAKE WITH SOUR-CREAM ICING

For some reason, this is the only chocolate cake my daughter likes. Obviously, she has more sophisticated tastes than her mother.

It comes by way of, but not entirely from, the great American cake-maker Rose Levy Beranbaum, and the sour cream provides a wonderful mouth-filling smoothness.

for the cake:

200g plain flour

200g caster sugar

3/4 teaspoon baking powder

1/4 teaspoon bicarbonate of soda

1/2 teaspoon salt

200g soft unsalted butter

40g best cocoa

150ml sour cream

2 large eggs

1 1/2 teaspoons vanilla extract

2 x 20cm sandwich tins, buttered and lined

for the icing:

80g milk chocolate

80g dark chocolate

75g unsalted butter

125ml sour cream

1 teaspoon vanilla extract

1 tablespoon golden syrup

300g golden icing sugar, sieved (plus more if needed)

1/2 teaspoon hot water

Preheat the oven to 180°C/gas mark 4.

Combine the flour, sugar, baking powder, bicarb and salt in a large bowl. Then, using an electric mixer, add the butter. In a wide-mouthed measuring jug, whisk together the cocoa, sour cream, eggs and vanilla, then slowly add this cocoa mixture to the ingredients in the bowl, beating until thoroughly mixed.

Pour the batter into the prepared tins and bake for 30 minutes; when they're ready the cakes should be starting to shrink back from the edges of the tins. Leave for 10 minutes in their tins on racks, then turn out to cool.

To make the icing, melt the chocolate and butter in a microwave, or in a bowl over hot water. Let cool a little, then stir in the sour cream, vanilla and syrup. Add the sieved icing sugar and a little hot water, blending until smooth. When you've got the texture right – thick enough to cover but supple enough to spread, adding more icing sugar or water as required – you can ice the cakes.

Cut four strips of baking parchment and make an outline of a square with them on a flat plate. Sit one cake on top of the paper pieces, spread with icing, sit the second cake on top and use the rest of the icing to cover the top and sides. Leave spatula-smooth or swirl with a knife as you wish.

Serves 6–8.

STORE-CUPBOARD CHOCOLATE-ORANGE CAKE

This is a different sort of chocolate cake: the sort you can make in a few minutes once you get home from work. Hardly any trouble, and you've got a gorgeously aromatic cake either for pudding or just to eat, as supper in its entirety, in front of the television. I think of it as a larder-standby because I tend to have all the ingredients in the house at any given time and if I don't the local corner shop stocks them all.

Even if you don't like marmalade, you should try this: all you taste is orange. Lisa Grillo, who is one of my chief guinea pigs, Italian, and thinks marmalade is a peculiar British perversion, loves it.

125g unsalted butter

100g dark chocolate, broken into
  pieces

300g good, thin-cut marmalade

150g caster sugar

pinch of salt

2 large eggs, beaten

150g self-raising flour

20cm Springform tin, buttered and
  floured

Preheat the oven to 180°C/gas mark 4.

Put the butter in a heavy-bottomed saucepan and put over a low heat to melt. When it's nearly completely melted, stir in the chocolate. Leave for a moment to begin softening, then take the pan off the heat and stir with a wooden spoon until the butter and chocolate are smooth and melted. Now add the marmalade, sugar, salt and eggs. Stir with your wooden spoon and when all is pretty well amalgamated, beat in the flour bit by bit. Put into your prepared tin and bake for about 50 minutes or until a cake-tester or skewer comes out clean. Cool in the pan on a rack for 10 minutes before turning out.

You can eat this still slightly warm (with crème fraîche, perhaps) or cold. For what it's worth, I haven't yet cooked it without someone asking for the recipe. It is, however, a plain-looking cake, and although I have no objection to that, if you want something slightly more elaborate, you could just dust it with icing sugar pushed through a tea strainer (and obviously this goes for all cakes); and if you wanted to go one further, get a cake stencil (which you can you buy in packets containing a few designs, decorative or seasonal), stick on masking tape handles (imperative if you're to lift the stencil off the cake without blurring your design), place on the cake and dust the icing sugar on top. I am particularly partial to the star and leaf designs – and I don't care who knows it.

Serves 6.

VARIATIONS

As I've already said, you can substitute the jam of your choice, and I'd suggest, first off, raspberry or apricot; but you should also consider making this with the marmalade's weight in dark, aromatic and velvety prune purée, which supermarkets tend to sell now, either in their upmarket-larder bits or in the baking aisle. If you're going for this prune-thick chocolate cake, serve with crème fraîche to which you've added a few crucial drops of Armagnac; indeed, you could add a slug to the cake too, or just pour a little over as soon as you unmould it.

CHOCOLATE-CHESTNUT CAKE

This is a seriously compelling piece of cake-bakery: definitely pudding – and an elegant one at that – rather than afternoon tea, though I think I might be able to force a slice down with a cup of coffee at unscheduled moments in the day. Really, you need serve nothing with it: apart from anything else, it's not so sweet as to need the masking properties of cream.

435g tin unsweetened chestnut purée
125g soft unsalted butter
1 teaspoon vanilla extract
1 tablespoon dark rum
6 large eggs, separated
250g melted chocolate

pinch of salt
50g caster sugar
25g light muscovado sugar
22cm Springform tin, greased
 and lined

Preheat the oven to 180°C/gas mark 4.

Beat the chestnut purée with the butter, then add the vanilla, rum, egg yolks and melted chocolate, blending well. I use my KitchenAid here, but an ordinary electric hand-held mixer would be fine – or even a bowl and wooden spoon. In another large bowl, whip the egg whites with the salt until they are foamy. Add the caster sugar gradually to form stiffer, glossy peaks, and then sprinkle the muscovado sugar over and either fold in or whisk in slowly. Fold the whites, gently but confidently, into the chestnut mixture, a third at a time.

Pour into the tin and cook for 45 minutes, until the cake has risen and is firm on top; it will look dry and cracked, but don't panic: it won't taste dry, and the cracks don't matter a damn.

Cool in the tin for 20 minutes, and then turn out on a rack.

When you want to eat it, dust with icing sugar and serve with modest pride.

Serves 8–10.

TORTA ALLA GIANDUIA

Or, less fancily, Nutella Cake. This is a fabulously easy cake, another that I draw into service for birthdays: the hazelnuts on top somehow give it a burnished, ceremonial look.

Please don't feel obliged to rush out and buy a bottle of Frangelico, the most divinely déclassé hazelnut liqueur, its monkish derivation signalled by the rope that is hung from the holy-brother-shaped bottle.

I use hazelnuts bought ready-ground, but ones you grind yourself in the processor will provide more nutty moistness.

for the cake:

6 large eggs, separated
pinch of salt
125g soft unsalted butter
400g Nutella (1 large jar)
1 tablespoon Frangelico, rum or water
100g ground hazelnuts
100g dark chocolate, melted

23cm Springform tin, greased and lined

for the icing:

100g hazelnuts (peeled weight)
125ml double cream
1 tablespoon Frangelico, rum or water
125g dark chocolate

Preheat the oven to 180°C/gas mark 4.

In a large bowl, whisk the egg whites and salt until stiff but not dry. In a separate bowl, beat the butter and Nutella together, and then add the Frangelico (or whatever you're using), egg yolks and ground hazelnuts. Fold in the cooled, melted chocolate, then lighten the mixture with a large dollop of egg white, which you can beat in as roughly as you want, before gently folding the rest of them in a third at a time. Pour into the prepared tin and cook for 40 minutes or until the cake's beginning to come away at the sides, then let cool on a rack.

Toast the hazelnuts in a dry frying pan until the aroma wafts upwards and the nuts are golden-brown in parts: keep shaking the pan so that they don't burn on one side and stay too pallid on others. Transfer to a plate and let cool. This is imperative: if they go on the ganache while hot, it'll turn oily. (Believe me, I speak from experience.)

In a heavy-bottomed saucepan, add the cream, liqueur or water and chopped chocolate, and heat gently. Once the chocolate's melted, take the pan off the heat and whisk until it reaches the right consistency to ice the top of the cake. Unmould the cooled cake carefully, leaving it on the base as it will be too difficult to get such a damp cake off in one piece. Ice the top with the chocolate icing, and dot thickly with the whole, toasted hazelnuts.

If you have used Frangelico, put shot glasses on the table and serve it with the cake. Serves 8.

GOOEY CHOCOLATE STACK

This is for those days or evenings when you want to usher a little something out of the kitchen that makes you thrill at the sheer pleasure you've conjured up. It isn't about showing off, it's about intensity: meringue that's marshmallow-gungy within and chewily crisp without, cocoa-flecked and feathery light; together with a slick, glossy crème patissière into which you've stirred the darkest of dark chocolates. I didn't think I believed in such things, but this is it: chocolate heaven.

Don't panic at the idea of crème patissière. It could hardly be easier: remember that the flour stabilizes it, so you don't have the knife-edge worry of its splitting; plus it's made in advance, as are the pavlova layers, so that it's just a simple stacking operation at the end.

You don't need to use the chopped pistachios I've suggested to scatter over the top: hazelnuts, almonds, indeed any nuts, would be fine; or you could go divinely retro with crystallized violets.

for the meringue discs:
6 large egg whites
300g golden caster sugar
3 tablespoons cocoa powder
1 teaspoon red wine vinegar
3 baking sheets

for the crème patissière:
6 large egg yolks

100g golden caster sugar
2 tablespoons cocoa powder
2 tablespoons plain flour
300ml full-fat milk
300ml double cream
100g the best dark chocolate, melted
1 teaspoon vanilla extract
20g pistachios, chopped

Preheat the oven to 140°C/gas mark 1.

Line the baking sheets with parchment and draw a 20cm circle on each one. The simplest way to do this is simply to find a bowl or cake tin with the desired dimensions, plonk it on and draw round it.

Whisk the egg whites until stiff, then add the sugar a spoonful at a time, beating in well after each addition. Believe me – and I speak as someone often criminally impatient – it does make life easier to go slowly here. Sprinkle over the cocoa and vinegar and then fold in gently but firmly.

Divide the dusky meringue between the 3 circles, spreading evenly. You don't need to worry too much about beating the air out of them as you smooth; I find they withstand a modicum of brutality.

Cook for 1 hour, then turn off the oven, leaving the meringues in until cool. Often, I just make them before I go to bed and leave them in the switched-off oven overnight. It makes for less hanging about. And as long as you keep them airtight, with

PAIN-AU-CHOCOLAT PUDDING

Of course you can make a thoroughly chocolate bread-and-butter pudding, either by adding melted chocolate or cocoa to the eggy custard, or simply by using a sliced-up chocolate loaf. But if you ask me, you're better off with this gentler, subtler take on what a chocolate bread-and-butter pudding might be: all I've done is slice up some stale pains au chocolat. It looks beautiful and tastes divine.

If you want to, by all means replace the 500ml each of double cream and milk with 1 litre of single cream.

3–4 stale pains au chocolat
500ml milk
500ml double cream
3 tablespoons caster sugar
1 large egg

4 large egg yolks
1/2 teaspoon vanilla extract
ovenproof dish with a capacity of
approximately 1 1/2 litres

Preheat the oven to 160°C/gas mark 3.

Butter your ovenproof dish (I always use one of those old-fashioned oval creamware dishes), cut up the pains au chocolat – I cut rough slices of about a centimetre – and arrange them in the dish. Put the milk and cream into a pan and bring near to boiling point. Whisk the egg, the yolks and the sugar in a large wide-mouthed measuring jug. When the milk and cream are nearly boiling, pour over the eggs and sugar, whisking continuously. Add the vanilla and then pour over the slices of pain au chocolat and leave to soak for 10 minutes.

Transfer to the preheated oven and cook for about 45 minutes, or until the pudding is softly set. I can't tell you how comforting this is.

Serves 6.

BROWNIES

I don't understand why people don't make brownies all the time – they're so easy and so wonderful. My friend Justine Picardie gave me the idea for setting the brownies so gloriously alight when she asked me to make them for her husband's birthday. Ever since then, I've copied the idea: brownies are much quicker to make than a cake, and they look so wonderful piled up in a rough-and-tumble pyramid spiked with birthday candles. And I'd much rather eat a brownie than a piece of birthday cake any day; I think most people would.

375g soft unsalted butter
375g best-quality dark chocolate
6 large eggs
1 tablespoon vanilla extract
500g caster sugar
225g plain flour

1 teaspoon salt
300g chopped walnuts
tin measuring approximately 33 x 23 x 5 1/2cm
birthday candles and holders, if appropriate

Preheat the oven to 180°C/gas mark 4. Line your brownie pan – I think it's worth lining the sides as well as the base – with foil, parchment or Bake-O-Glide.

Melt the butter and chocolate together in a large heavy-based pan. In a bowl or large wide-mouthed measuring jug, beat the eggs with the sugar and vanilla. Measure the flour into another bowl and add the salt.

When the chocolate mixture has melted, let it cool a bit before beating in the eggs and sugar, and then the nuts and flour. Beat to combine smoothly and then scrape out of the saucepan into the lined pan.

Bake for about 25 minutes. When it's ready, the top should be dried to a paler brown speckle, but the middle still dark and dense and gooey. And even with such a big batch you do need to keep alert, keep checking: the difference between gungy brownies and dry brownies is only a few minutes; remember that they will continue to cook as they cool.

Makes a maximum of 48.

VARIATIONS
You can really vary brownies as you wish: get rid of the walnuts, or halve them and make up their full weight with dried cherries; or replace them with other nuts – peanuts, brazils, hazelnuts – add shredded coconut or white chocolate chips or buttons; try stirring in some Jordan's Original Crunchy cereal. I had high hopes for chic, after-dinner pistachio-studded brownies, but found the nuts get too soft and waxy, when what you need is a little crunchy contrast.

CHOCOLATE-CHERRY CUPCAKES

These are very easy, very good – somehow light and dense at the same time – and I love their dark, glossy elegance. When I made them for the cake stall at my daughter's school fair, they sold, even at a pound a piece, quicker than anything else. I'd have included them in the school fête section (see p235), except that they're perhaps too expensive to make a habit of. Still, if the cost considerations include time, then this probably counts as a cheap undertaking.

The jam I use for these is the morello cherry preserve from Sainsbury's special selection; if you're using a less elegant, and probably sweeter confection, reduce the sugar in the cakes a little. And if you have any Kirsch about the place, then add a splash to the batter and icing.

for the cupcakes:

125g soft unsalted butter

100g dark chocolate, broken into pieces

300g morello cherry jam

150g caster sugar

pinch of salt

2 large eggs, beaten

150g self-raising flour

12-bun muffin tin and papers

for the icing:

100g dark chocolate

100ml double cream

12 natural-coloured glacé cherries

Preheat the oven to 180°C/gas mark 4.

Put the butter in a heavy-bottomed pan on the heat to melt. When nearly completely melted, stir in the chocolate. Leave for a moment to begin softening, then take the pan off the heat and stir with a wooden spoon until the butter and chocolate are smooth and melted. Now add the cherry jam, sugar, salt and eggs. Stir with a wooden spoon and when all is pretty well amalgamated stir in the flour.

Scrape and pour into the muffin papers in their tin and bake for 25 minutes. Cool in the pan on a rack for 10 minutes before turning out.

When the cupcakes are cool, break the chocolate for the icing into little pieces and add them to the cream in a saucepan. Bring to the boil, remove from the heat and then whisk – by hand or electrically – till thick and smooth. Ice the cupcakes, smoothing the tops with the back of a spoon, and stand a cherry in the centre of each.

Makes 12.

FLORENTINES

This is the one recipe using glacé cherries in which I won't beseech you to use the dark natural-coloured ones; we want that garish, chemical red here. I won't claim this isn't a fiddly recipe, but you need patience rather than dexterity or expertise, and they are so good it would be a pity if you never found the calmness from which to produce them. Hettie, who's worked with me on this book, customarily calls me Frank, as in Spencer, and if I can make these, so can you. These taste so much better than any florentines you've ever bought.

100g whole, blanched almonds
90g mixed candied peel, in whole
chunks, not ready chopped
40g glacé cherries
25g unsalted butter
90g caster sugar

15g plain flour
150ml double cream
100g dark chocolate
100g white chocolate
2 baking sheets, greased

Preheat the oven to 190°C/gas mark 5.

Chop the almonds so that you have some fine pieces and some chunks of nut. Chop the candied peel and cherries into fairly small, even pieces. In a heavy-based saucepan, melt the butter and sugar without letting it catch. Add the flour rather as if you were making a roux for a white sauce; it should form a ball of paste. Take off the heat and whisk in the cream. The mixture should be smooth, so put it back on the heat briefly to beat out any lumps. Stir in the fruit and almonds.

Drop heaped teaspoonfuls of this florentine mixture onto the greased or non-stick baking sheets. It will look quite liquid and will spread, so leave generous space between the blobs. Place the sheets in the oven and cook for 10–12 minutes. They're ready when they've spread into larger circles and the edges are golden-brown. Take them out of the oven and leave for 2–3 minutes to firm up; at this point you can ease them back into shape if you need to, as they will be very malleable. When you feel they can be lifted, slip a metal spatula or palette knife underneath them and transfer to a wire rack to cool, ensuring you leave them flat.

Melt the dark and white chocolate in separate bowls in the microwave, and paint the flat side of each florentine; I use a pastry brush for this. Be prepared to paint over and over to get a good thick coating, although it's more of an issue with the white chocolate.

Using a fork, make wavy lines on the chocolate on each florentine, and leave to dry.

Makes approximately 30.

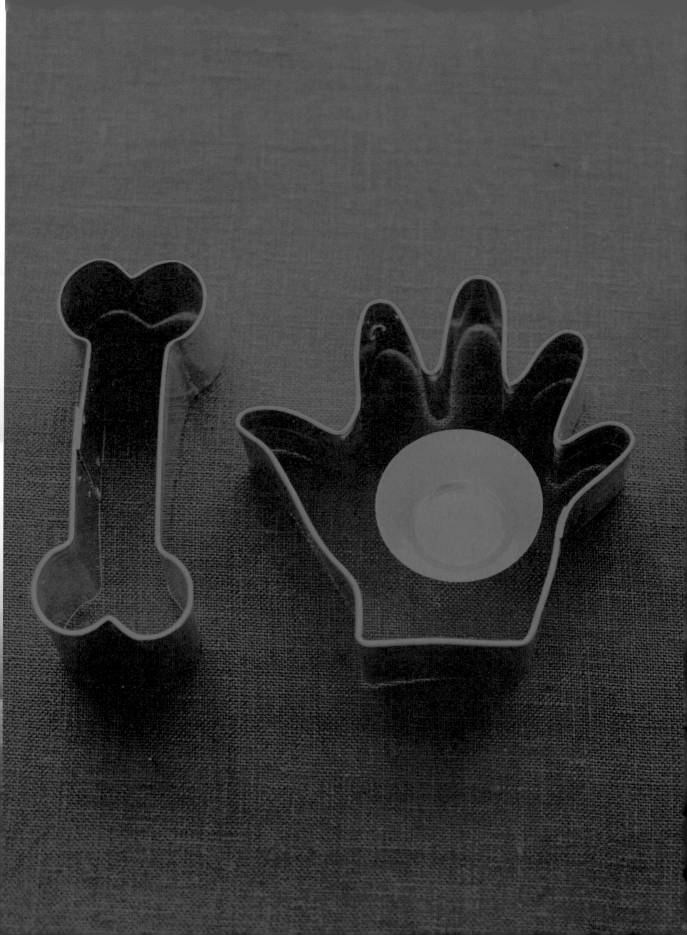

CHILDREN

CHILDREN

Although in cooking I resist strongly the idea that there is such a thing as children's food, as distinct from 'real' food, in baking I have, I suppose, to lighten up. Not that I think that peanut-butter squares are therefore unfit for adult consumption – sadly, that doesn't appear to be the case – or that dolly-mixture cupcakes cannot lie happily with a child-free life, but they are both the sort of thing I have in mind when I talk about baking for children. Indeed, many of the recipes here can be made by children, too, although it would be hard to make a useful distinction throughout the chapter between cooking for and cooking with children – that would inevitably depend on their age. And actually, so much of children's baking isn't about what they can be left alone to get on with, but about what you do together. I love hanging around the kitchen with the children, stirring mixtures, licking out bowls, baking fairy cakes or cutting out and icing biscuits. But it's also incredibly important to me that that doesn't usurp everyday cooking; I like them with me in the kitchen helping – or not, as the case may be – with ordinary lunch or tea, not just on-side for kiddie cuisine. In fact, even though I'm lucky enough to work at home, I'm hopelessly negligent and never actually do much with my children other than cook.

BUTTER CUT-OUT BISCUITS

It's not hard to make biscuits that hold their shape well while cooking; it's not hard to make biscuits that taste good and have a melting, buttery texture: what's hard is to find a biscuit that does all of these things together. This one, by way of a wonderful American book, *The Family Baker*, does: so any time you want to play supermummy in the kitchen, here is where you start.

Like all doughs, it freezes well, so it makes sense – in a smug, domestic kind of a way – to wrap half of this in clingfilm and stash it in the deep freeze until next needed. It's hard to specify exactly how much icing you'll need, but you might end up using more than specified below if you're using a lot of different colours. I always cut out the newly acquired age of the child on his or her birthday. My children couldn't contemplate a birthday party without them.

175g soft unsalted butter	**1 teaspoon baking powder**
200g caster sugar	**1 teaspoon salt**
2 large eggs	**300g icing sugar, sieved, and food**
1 teaspoon vanilla extract	**colouring**
400g plain flour, preferably Italian 00,	biscuit cutters
plus more if needed	2 baking sheets, greased or lined

Preheat the oven to 180°C/gas mark 4.

Cream the butter and sugar together until pale and moving towards moussiness, then beat in the eggs and vanilla. In another bowl, combine the flour, baking powder and salt. Add the dry ingredients to the butter and eggs, and mix gently but surely. If you think the finished mixture is too sticky to be rolled out, add more flour, but do so sparingly as too much will make the dough tough. Halve the dough, form into fat discs, wrap each half in clingfilm and rest in the fridge for at least 1 hour. Sprinkle a suitable surface with flour, place a disc of dough on it (not taking out the other half until you've finished with the first) and sprinkle a little more flour on top of that. Then roll it out to a thickness of about ½ cm. Cut into shapes, dipping the cutter into flour as you go, and place the biscuits a little apart on the baking sheets.

Bake for 8–12 minutes, by which time they will be lightly golden around the edges. Cool on a rack and continue with the rest of the dough. When they're all fully cooled, you can get on with the icing. Put a couple of tablespoons of just-not-boiling water into a large bowl, add the sieved icing sugar and mix together, adding more water as you need to form a thick paste. Colour as desired: let the artistic spirit within you speak, remembering with gratitude that children have very bad taste.

Makes 50–60.

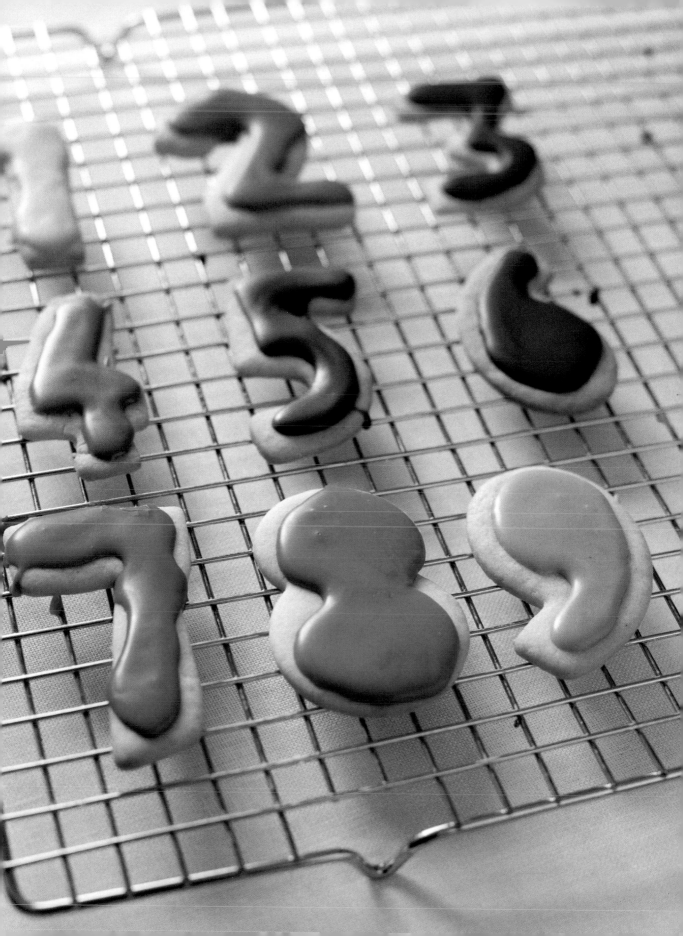

BIRTHDAY-PARTY AND CHILD-FRIENDLY FAIRY CAKES

Fairy cakes that you make for a child are no different from the cupcakes with which you adorn your dinner-party table (pp39–42); that's partly the point. I would say one thing, though: you should always keep some Stork, or similar, in the fridge so that you can make up a quick batch whenever necessary. (OK, I'm not mad on margarine, either, but I promise you this is an accommodation that makes sense.) Butter just won't soften quickly; the Stork you can bung straight from fridge to processor, and thus you are never more than about 20 minutes away from a tray of fairy cakes.

TRADITIONAL FAIRY CAKES

To make 12 fairy cakes, use the recipe on p40 and ice with pink icing, using 200g icing sugar (or instant royal icing), a tablespoonful or so of water, pink food colouring and 12 natural-coloured or shriekingly artificial glacé cherries.

DOLLY-MIXTURE FAIRY CAKES

All children love these and I find them curiously therapeutic to make. Choosing the patterns and sticking down the sugary cubes is entirely absorbing without being in any way demanding. Two packs of sweets make for leftovers but artistic freedom. So important.

for the cakes:
as on p40

for the icing:
**250g instant royal (and you may need
    more if you're using lots of colours)
colouring of your choice
2 x 125g packets dolly mixtures**

Use the regular recipe for cakes, cutting any risen bit of cake off so you've got a flat surface to adorn. Make up the icing, following packet instructions. Dollop a tablespoonful or so into a bowl, add the colouring of your choice (I enjoy a bit of mix-and-match artistry here) and blend. Ice the cake in question, smooth with the back of an ordinary dessert spoon, and leave a few minutes before studding with dolly mixtures. If you decorate before the icing is beginning to dry, the dolly mixtures will slide off.

    Makes 12.

SNICKERS AND PEANUT-BUTTER MUFFINS

These muffins have a special charm: I think the ingredients speak for themselves. But what I should perhaps add is that they taste seriously good to adults too.

250g plain flour
6 tablespoons golden caster sugar
(85g)
1 ½ tablespoons baking powder
pinch of salt
6 tablespoons crunchy peanut butter
(160g)

60g unsalted butter, melted
1 large egg, beaten
175ml milk
3 x 65g Snickers bars, chopped
12-bun muffin tin with paper cases

Preheat the oven to 200°C/gas mark 6.

Stir together the flour, sugar, baking powder and salt. Add the peanut butter and mix until you have a bowl of coarse crumbs. Add the melted butter and egg to the milk, and then stir this gently into the bowl. Mix in the Snickers pieces and dollop into the muffin cases.

Cook for 20–25 minutes, when the tops should be risen, golden and firm to the (light) touch. Sit the tin on a wire rack for 5–10 minutes before taking out each muffin in its case and leaving them on the wire rack to cool. If you can.

Makes 12.

BANANA MUFFINS

Any sort of muffin is easy and quick for a child to make: the whole point is that the mixture must not be too vehemently or smoothly combined. The bonus here is that small children seem to have an inordinate passion for mashing bananas. In other words, an ordinarily biddable two-year-old can feel he or she is making these almost unaided. You will have to melt the butter and so on yourself, but – although I am perhaps irresponsibly insouciant about infantile involvement here – on the whole, you can take a serenely non-interventionist approach to the whole exercise.

All the ingredients can be bought at any unglamorously stocked corner shop, as can the ingredients for the recipe below. It doesn't matter whether you use mini-muffin tins or full-size ones: you will get about 24 of the former, 10 of the latter. For what it's worth, the tiny ones taste better when eaten still warm; the larger ones when cold. Just remember to buy the right-sized lining papers for whichever tins you've got.

Snickers and peanut-butter muffins

As soon as you've taken the biscuits out of the oven, spoon a small amount of jam (about a coffee-spoonful) into each indent to make a jewel. Transfer them to a wire rack to cool, by which time the jam will have melted slightly, and will be sitting, bulging shinily, a red gem in the middle of its peanut-butter setting. The jam seems to harden slightly, not enough to make it unpleasant but enough to make it stay put, so you can pack these up, on top of each other, in tins or Tupperwares, without their coming to any harm.

Makes about 50.

PEANUT-BUTTER SQUARES

I don't know if you've ever eaten Reese's Peanut Butter Cups, but these are a homespun version of them. And if you discount melting the chocolate (which in any case the microwave can do) there is no cooking involved. You may think that seeing how the dough is made – just peanut butter, butter and sugar – might put you off eating them. Sadly not.

for the base:
50g dark muscovado sugar
200g icing sugar
50g unsalted butter
200g smooth peanut butter

for the topping:
200g milk chocolate
100g plain chocolate
1 tablespoon unsalted butter
1 x 23cm square brownie tin, lined,
preferably, with Bake-O-Glide

Stir all the ingredients for the base together until smooth. I use the paddle attachment to my mixer which my children love operating, but a bowl and a wooden spoon will do the job just as well. You will find, either way, that some of the dark muscovado sugar stays in rubbly, though very small, lumps, but don't worry about that. Press the sandy mixture into the lined brownie tin and make the surface as even as possible.

To make the topping, melt the chocolates and butter together (in a microwave for ease, for a minute or two on medium) and spread on the base. Put the tin in the fridge to set. When the chocolate has hardened, cut into small squares – because, more-ish as it undeniably is, it is also very rich.

Makes approximately 48.

ROCKY ROAD

Ever since I read that brazil nuts are inordinately good for you, containing essential selenium, and that you should probably have three a day, I have chosen to regard these as health food. What they really are are clumps of brazil nuts and mini-marshmallows bound together by a mantle of melted chocolate. You can alter the ratio of dark to light chocolate as you wish, but, as ever, I really do think it's worth using the best chocolate that you can.

200g milk chocolate
25g dark chocolate
75g brazil nuts
75g mini-marshmallows

1 baking sheet, lined with greaseproof, Bake-O-Glide or oiled foil

Melt the chocolates either in the microwave or using a bowl over a pan of barely simmering water. Roughly chop the brazil nuts, and mix into the chocolate with the mini-marshmallows.

Drop heaped teaspoons onto a lined baking sheet, and leave to cool in a cold place, though not the fridge if at all possible; it will take some of the gleam from the chocolate.

Makes 24.

VARIATION
You could chop these up and stir into slightly softened vanilla or chocolate ice cream.

EASTER NESTS

Yes, these are cute; yes, they are kitsch, but I love them all the same. Can't say I'm absolutely mad about eating them, but luckily my children are.

200g milk chocolate
25g dark chocolate
25g unsalted butter
100g shredded wheat

about 25 multicoloured sugar-coated little chocolate eggs
1 baking sheet, lined with Bake-O-Glide or oiled foil

Break up the chocolate into small pieces and put it in a glass bowl with the butter. Melt on a medium heat in the microwave for about 2 minutes – I give it a minute, then look to see how much more it might need – or over water. When it's melted, give it a stir, then leave it to one side for a moment or two. You need it to be a bit cooler or it might burn the children's hands. Crumble the shredded wheat into another bowl.

Now mix the contents of the two bowls and remove a small handful of messy mixture to the lined baking tray and form into a round nest shape, about 7cm in diameter. Don't worry if you feel it won't stick together: it will as it cools. Leave in a cool place (though not the fridge) until set, then remove to a plate or a wooden board and fill the centre with the eggs (about 5 per nest).

Makes 5.

MERINGUES (AND MERINGUE NESTS)

I've never met a child who didn't like meringues, and they're child's play to make, too. The best way of getting meringue-making fixed into your (or your child's) head is to remember that for each egg white you need 60g caster sugar, and that this in turn will make you around ten 6cm-diameter meringues. For this reason, I give method only:

Preheat the oven to 140°C/gas mark 1.

Whisk the egg white(s) till stiff, but not dry; peaks should be firm and hold their shape. Resume whisking, adding the sugar tablespoon by sprinkled tablespoon till all's incorporated and you have a gleaming, satiny mass. You can pipe meringues onto lined (but not greased) baking trays, but I mound dessertspoonfuls onto the trays and then use the back of the spoon, wiggling it around so that I have neat-nippled, small-bosomed shapes. To make nests, simply use the back of the spoon to make a nest shape. Bake for 60–70 minutes, then leave in the switched-off oven for 20 minutes before removing to cool.

MINI-PAVLOVAS

Because of the fruit – and the cream, for that matter – these are not cheap to make, but I always have a stash of egg whites in my deep freeze so I reckon I'm halfway there before I start. And actually, you can probably sell them for quite a lot too. You need to make sure that you've got a supply of paper plates and napkins, though, as they're not small enough to eat in one neat mouthful.

What I do is take with me a large Tupperware of meringues, another airtight bowl of the whipped double cream and, in another, or still in their punnets, the berries. I also bring with me my tea-strainer, a teaspoon, a packet of icing sugar, paper plates and little plastic forks. When I arrive at my pitch, I set out the meringue bases, dollop the cream on top, arrange the fruit and dust with icing sugar, being ready to top up from time to time as the sugar dissolves into the berries. It's a palaver, but worth it: they look so pretty people can't stop themselves spending whatever extortionate price you've put on them.

8 large egg whites
pinch of salt
500g caster sugar
4 teaspoons cornflour
1 scant teaspoon vanilla extract
2 teaspoons white wine vinegar

750ml whipping cream, duly whipped
750g blackberries
750g raspberries
icing sugar for dusting

3 baking sheets, lined with parchment
tea-strainer

Preheat the oven to 180°C/gas mark 4.

Whisk the egg whites with the salt until they're holding firm peaks but are not stiff. Gently add in the sugar, spoonful after spoonful, still beating, until you've got a bowl full of gleaming, satiny, snowy meringue. Sprinkle the cornflour, a few drops of vanilla and the vinegar on top and fold in to combine.

Draw 6 circles of approximately 10cm circles (using a pint glass as a guide, if this helps) on each of the parchment-lined sheets. Spoon the meringue onto the baking parchment into the delineated circles, and spread and smooth to fill. You want to make the meringue slightly higher at the rims, or just use the back of the spoon to make an indentation in the centre to hold the cream and fruit later. Put into the oven, turn it down to 150°C/gas mark 2, and bake for 30 minutes. Turn the oven off and leave them in for another 30 minutes, then take out of the oven to cool. I just transfer them, on their baking parchment, to wire racks. When you want to assemble them, dollop cream into the indentation, and smooth it with the back of a spoon, leaving the odd peak. Place, one by one, a few blackberries and a few raspberries so that they look well filled but not crammed. Dust with icing sugar.

Makes 18.

MINI LIME-SYRUP SPONGES

This is really just the miniaturization of the lemon-syrup sponge on p13. You could do them in lemon here, too, or use a mixture of ordinary orange juice and lime juice to evoke the wonderful acerbity of Seville oranges. (Or indeed use those when in season.) It doesn't matter what the citrus is: there is just something about these small-scale, perfectly formed loaves that make them particularly appealing.

125g unsalted butter, softened
175g caster sugar
2 large eggs
zest of 1 lime
175g self-raising flour
pinch of salt
4 tablespoons milk

8-bun mini-loaf tin, buttered very well

for the syrup:
4 tablespoons lime juice (of 1–2 limes), plus zest for decoration
100g icing sugar

Preheat the oven to 180°C/gas mark 4.

Cream together the butter and sugar, and add the eggs and lime zest, beating them in well. Add the flour and salt, folding in gently, and then the milk. Spoon into the mini-loaf tin, and cook for 25 minutes.

While the cakes are cooking, prepare the syrup by putting the lime juice and sugar into a small saucepan and heating gently so that the sugar dissolves.

As soon as the mini-sponges are ready, take them out of the oven and prick them with a cake-tester all over. Pour over the syrup evenly. Try to let the middle absorb the liquid as well as the sides, then leave it to soak up the rest. Don't try to take the cakes out of the tin until they have cooled slightly and the syrup looks like it has been absorbed, but be aware that if you leave these to go completely cold they might be very difficult to get out of the tin.

So, after an hour or two, turn them out onto a rack and grate some lime zest over them before serving (or selling).

Makes 8.

CHRISTMAS

CHRISTMAS

I think it is probably the case that even people who never, ever bake might consider doing so at Christmas. This doesn't mean I'm going to load you down with homework, presenting this chapter as a kind of holiday-season project; the real point is that at Christmas you might feel you've got more time to play around with some of these recipes (or indeed any of the recipes in this book).

I must emphasize that, having never been someone to bake her own Christmas cake, make her own Christmas pudding, it is deeply satisfying when you do. This doesn't mean it has to become a yearly obligation, a source of pressure rather than pleasure. One of the best things about being adult is that you can decide which rituals and ceremonies you want to adopt to give shape to your life and which you want to lose because they just constrain you. True, I think it takes more determination to shuck off the habits that you've inherited but don't actually want at Christmas time; it's hard not to feel that the way you always did it when you were a child is the way it should be done. So, I've consciously enjoyed setting my own pattern here, choosing what I want to be part of my family's Christmas.

You surely know by now that, as ever, what follows is suggestion, not instruction.

CHRISTMAS CAKE

I think you do need to have a blueprint for a basic fruit cake that you can make up in whatever size you need. I've already given you recipes from Hettie Potter, who's worked with me on this book; she gave me this, too, from her brother-in-law's mother, Hazel, in New Zealand. The only change I make is to ignore the suggestion of brandy or sherry in favour of Marsala. You do entirely as you wish.

As with all rich fruit cakes, this should be made at least 3–4 weeks before you plan to eat it. And the actual preparation does have its *Blue Peter* moments – you'll need brown paper, as well as baking parchment, to line the tin and stop the cake from scorching.

Place all of the fruit in a large bowl, and add the brandy or sherry. Cover and let the fruit soak overnight.

Preheat your oven to 150°C/gas mark 2. Line your tin with a double thickness of brown paper, then line again with baking parchment, both to come up a good 10cm above the rim of the tin.

Cream the butter and sugar, then beat in the orange and lemon zest. Add the eggs one at a time, beating well after each addition, and then the marmalade. Sift the dry ingredients together, then mix the fruit alternately with the dry ingredients into the creamed mixture. Add the almond essence and combine thoroughly.

Put the cake mix into the prepared tin and bake following the table above, or until a cake-tester comes out clean.

When the cake is cooked, brush with a couple of tablespoons of extra liqueur. Wrap immediately in its tin – using a double-thickness of tin foil – as this will trap the heat and form steam, which in turn will keep the cake soft on top. When it's completely cold, remove the cake from the tin and rewrap in foil, storing, preferably in an airtight tin or Tupperware, for at least 3 weeks.

For icing, see my comments in the recipe for black cake below (p250).

	110g (¹/₄lb)	225g (¹/₂lb)	350g (³/₄lb)
sultanas	350g	700g	1kg
raisins	110g	225g	350g
currants	50g	110g	175g
glacé cherries	50g	110g	175g
mixed peel	50g	110g	175g
brandy or sherry	60ml	120ml	180ml
butter	110g	225g	350g
brown sugar	90g	195g	300g
orange zest, grated	¹/₃ teaspoon	1 teaspoon	1¹/₂ teaspoon
lemon zest, grated	¹/₂ teaspoon	1 teaspoon	1¹/₂ teaspoon
large eggs	2	4	6
marmalade	1 tablespoon	2 tablespoons	3 tablespoons
plain flour	250g	350g	525g
mixed spice	¹/₂ teaspoon	1 teaspoon	1¹/₂ teaspoons
cinnamon	pinch	¹/₄ teaspoon	¹/₄ teaspoon
nutmeg	pinch	¹/₄ teaspoon	¹/₄ teaspoon
almond essence	¹/₂ teaspoon	1 teaspoon	1 teaspoon
salt	pinch	pinch	¹/₄ teaspoon
tin: round	18cm	23cm	25¹/₂cm
or square	15cm	20cm	23cm
temperature	150°C/gas mark 2	150°C/gas mark 2	150°C/gas mark 2, reduce to 140°C/gas mark 1 after 1 hour
cooking time	2–2¹/₂ hours	3–3¹/₂ hours	4–4¹/₂ hours

BLACK CAKE

This recipe comes from one of my favourite books, Laurie Colwin's *Home Cooking*. There are few food books that have such genuineness of tone, such love of food and of life. Laurie Colwin died young, and I often think of her family, her daughter, whom she writes about with such passion and interest. It's an extraordinarily powerful legacy that she's left her.

This cake was introduced to Laurie Colwin by her daughter's West Indian babysitter: 'Its closest relatives are plum pudding and black bun, but it leaves both in the dust. Black cake, like truffles and vintage Burgundy, is deep, complicated and intense. It has taste and aftertaste. It demands to be eaten in a slow, meditative way. The texture is complicated, too – dense and light at the same time.' Here is the recipe, altered only slightly by me.

for the fruit:

250g raisins

250g prunes

250g currants

250g natural-coloured glacé cherries

165g mixed peel (the real thing, not the chopped stuff in tubs)

1/2 bottle Madeira

1/2 bottle darkest rum you can find

Chop all the fruit very finely in the food processor. I advise you to go slowly, one fruit at a time, or else you'll find you've got purée.

Put the chopped fruit into a huge Tupperware and mix pleasurably and stickily with your hands to combine and then pour over the Madeira and rum. I should perhaps say that Laurie Colwin suggested Passover wine, but unless you're doing this around Easter/Passover you'll never find it; and Madeira is, I'm told, the best substitute for it.

Cover the fruits and leave to steep for at least two weeks, but up to six months. I say up to six months – which is what Colwin writes in *Home Cooking* – but I must tell you that I steeped all the fruits one year in November only to find in December that I was just too exhausted to make the cake. So I used it up the following year, after 13 months' marinating. It was strong, but it was good.

for the cake:

250g soft unsalted butter
250g dark muscovado sugar
the marinated fruit mixture
1/2 tablespoon vanilla extract
1/4 teaspoon freshly ground nutmeg
1/4 teaspoon ground cinnamon

6 large eggs
275g plain flour, preferably Italian 00
1 1/2 teaspoons baking powder
125g black treacle
deep, 23cm cake tin, lined as for
   Christmas cake, above

Preheat the oven to 180°C/gas mark 4.

Cream the butter and sugar, and beat in the fruit, rum and wine mixture. I use my KitchenAid free-standing mixer for this: it wouldn't be impossible to do by hand, but it takes a lot of muscle. Add the vanilla, nutmeg and cinnamon, and then beat in the eggs. Stir in the flour and baking powder, and finally the black treacle. The batter should be dark brown.

Pour this dark batter into the prepared tin and cook for 1 hour, then turn the oven down to 170°/gas mark 3 and cook for a further 2½–3 hours. Remove to a wire rack but do not unmould till the cake's completely cold, at which stage, wrap it in a double-thickness of foil and put it back in a Tupperware until you want to ice it.

for the icing:

1/2 jar marmalade (about 200g)
icing sugar for sprinkling

500g marzipan
1kg ready-to-roll icing
1 pair of holly-leaf cutters

I was teased mercilessly last year for proposing my white-on-white holly-decorated Christmas cake, but as precious as it sounds, it is simply beautiful. And I promise you those who at first mocked, ate their words and my cake.

I don't think there is anything better than an all-white cake – especially with an interior as dense and dark as this one's – but you could easily cut holly leaves out of dark green icing if you wanted. Holly-leaf cutters tend to come in pairs – a smaller and a larger leaf – complete with vein-stamping *truc*. The berries you have to roll yourself, but for this I suggest in any case you buy the icing ready to roll. Of course you can whisk sieved icing sugar with egg whites until it's the right consistency to roll out and ice, but the bought stuff, especially if it comes from a cake-decoration shop, is fine.

Heat the marmalade in a saucepan and when hot and runny strain into a bowl to remove rind. With a pastry brush, paint all over the cake to make a tacky surface. Dust a work surface with icing sugar, roll out the marzipan and drape over the cake. Then press against the cake and cut off the excess with a sharp knife. If you need to do this twice (with two lots of 250g marzipan), that's fine, but make sure to smooth over any joins, so that the icing on top lies smoothly. Dust the work surface again with icing sugar and plonk down your block of icing. Beat it a few times with the rolling pin, then dust the top with icing sugar and roll out. Cover the cake with it, again cutting off the excess and sticking bits together to patch up as you need, sprinkling with cold water first. Transfer the cake to a cake stand or board: once you've added the leaves you really don't want to move it again.

Re-roll the remaining icing and start stamping out the larger holly leaves (dipping the cutter into icing sugar first) and pressing down on them with the vein-stamper. Wet the underneath of each with a little cold water and stick onto the cake to form a circle about 3cm in from the cake's edge. Don't make all the holly leaves face the same way: you want this to look a bit like a holly wreath, which means that although most leaves should be placed aslant, they shouldn't be in a uniform ring. Now do the same with the smaller leaves, sticking them to make a circle around the base of the cake, in other words, blurring the line between cake board and cake. Make tiny balls, to resemble the berries, out of some of the icing that remains. Again, don't be uniform about the way you stick them on: put one berry between some leaves, a bunch of three between others, and so on.

SNOW-TOPPED SPICE CAKE

This cake – fruitless, light but aromatic – is the perfect replacement for the standard Christmas cake for those who hate it or just haven't got time to make it. The dripping blanket of royal icing certainly lends a seasonal touch, but the dark gingerbread spiciness is enough on its own if you'd prefer to keep it very simple.

I know the list of ingredients is long, but check out the method before deciding this is too labour-intensive: as you'll see, it's about the easiest cake you could make. And if you want to see what it looks like, give or take, turn to the picture of the chocolate-coffee volcano (p180); I use the same cake mould for both.

for the cake:

4 large eggs, separated, plus 2 extra large egg whites
125ml vegetable oil
125ml water
2 tablespoons runny honey
200g dark muscovado sugar
75g ground almonds
150g plain flour
2 teaspoons baking powder
1 teaspoon bicarbonate of soda

pinch of salt
1 teaspoon ground ginger
1 teaspoon cinnamon
1/2 teaspoon all-spice
1/4 teaspoon ground cloves
zest of 1/2 an orange
100g caster sugar
25cm Bundt tin, well buttered

for the icing:
250g instant royal icing

Preheat the oven to 180°C/gas mark 4.

Whisk together the yolks and oil, then add the water, honey and dark muscovado sugar. Add the almonds, flour, baking powder, bicarb, salt, spices and zest, folding in gently. In another bowl, beat the egg whites until soft peaks form and then gradually add the caster sugar. Fold the whites into the cake mixture, and pour into the Bundt tin. Cook for 45 minutes, or until the cake is springy on top and beginning to shrink away from the edges. Let the cake cool in its tin on a rack for 25 minutes before turning it out.

When it's completely cold, you can make up the icing. Put the icing sugar in a bowl with as much water as specified on the packet and whisk till thick. And you do need this to be thick, or else it will just melt into the damp stickiness of the cake. Use more icing if you want a thicker coating, but leave to dry before slicing.

CERTOSINO

This is the most fabulous Italian spicy fruit cake, decorated glossily with candied fruits and nuts, and best eaten in the tiniest slices with a glass of vin santo or, crossing continents for a moment, Australian black or orange muscat. I'm afraid I've taken terrible liberties with the recipe given to me by Anna del Conte; this is an anglicized version insofar as I've greatly augmented the apples to give a much wetter cake. I do think Italians appreciate a dry cake in the way that we don't. I've also, for purely personal reasons, got rid of the candied peel. As for the decorative topping: I've been vague about quantities because it depends completely on what you want to use and how.

75g seedless raisins

30ml Marsala

350g plain flour

2 teaspoons bicarbonate of soda

150g clear honey

150g caster sugar

40g unsalted butter

3 tablespoons water

1 tablespoon anise or fennel seeds

1 teaspoon ground cinnamon

375g Coxes apples (2 medium), roughly grated

200g blanched almonds, coarsely chopped

50g pine nuts

75g bitter chocolate, chopped

75g walnuts, chopped

25cm Springform cake tin, buttered and lined

suggestions for decorating:

4 tablespoons apricot jam to glaze

pecan halves

natural-coloured glacé cherries

blanched whole almonds

marrons glacés

glacé fruits

Soak the raisins in the Marsala for 20 minutes, and while they're steeping, preheat the oven to 180°C/gas mark 4. Measure the flour and bicarb out into a large bowl. Heat the honey, sugar, butter and water in a saucepan until the sugar dissolves. Add the anise or fennel seeds and cinnamon, pour this mixture over the bowl of flour and bicarb, and stir to combine.

Mix in all the other ingredients, not forgetting the soaked raisins and their liquid, then spoon into the tin and cook for ¾–1 hour; and should you find the cake needs that final 15 minutes, you may need to cover it with foil to stop it catching. When the cake has cooled, heat the apricot jam in a small pan and, using a pastry brush, paint most but not all of it over the top of the cake to glaze and give a sticky surface to which the fruits and so forth will adhere. Decorate with glacé fruits and nuts of your choice, leaving no gaps of cake visible on top. Brush with scant remaining glaze so all looks burnished and shiny.

pulsing till it looks as if the dough is about to cohere; you want to stop just before it does (even if some orange juice is left). If all your juice is used up and you need more liquid, add some iced water. Turn out of the processor and, in your hands, combine to a dough. Then form into two discs. Roll out one of the discs to make a rectangle approximately 40 x 32cm. Lay this on top of the tray, gently pushing the pastry down into the moulds with your fingertips. Give yourself a lot of slack. When you feel all the moulds are lined with pastry, take your rolling pin and roll over the top of the pastry to cut off the excess. When you take that away you should be left with 12 lined barquette moulds. Put this tray in the fridge for 20 minutes, preheating the oven to 200°C/gas mark 6 as you do so.

Empty the mincemeat into a bowl and stir in the ground cloves, orange zest and orange-flower water, then drop 2 scant teaspoons into each barquette mould, spreading it gently to fill. Add more if you want, but remember that the pastry sides will slip down as they bake. Either snip the filo into shreds with scissors or pinch off bits of the konafa and crumble over the mincemeat in the moulds. Drizzle the filo or konafa with the melted butter, transfer to the oven and bake for about 15 minutes, or until the pastry cases and filo topping are cooked and golden.

Remove from the oven and, using a palette knife, help the pies out of the tray and onto a wire rack to cool. When the barquette moulds are cold, start again with the second disc of pastry.

Dust with icing sugar pushed through a tea-strainer before serving.
Makes 24.

STAR-TOPPED MINCE PIES

Please don't think these will be better if you make the pastry out of butter rather than the butter and Trex mixed; it's the vegetable shortening which makes the pies so celestially light (though by all means use lard if you object to 'fake' fats). And it's the acid in the orange juice that makes the pastry especially tender.

240g plain flour, preferably Italian 00
60g Trex or other vegetable fat
60g cold unsalted butter
juice of 1 orange
pinch of salt
approximately 200g mincemeat
1 large egg, mixed with a tablespoon
    water, to glaze (optional)

icing sugar for dusting
tray of miniature tart tins, each indent
    4¹/₂cm in diameter
5¹/₂cm fluted round biscuit cutter
4cm star cutter

CHRISTMAS CUPCAKES

These beauties also make a very good alternative to mince pies. I buy the icing ready-made and dyed (which is why it isn't a very convincing colour for holly, let's be frank) and use cranberries as the holly berries. The cake underneath is somewhere between chocolate and gingerbread. If you're thinking of taking anything to friends' houses, may I suggest these?

150g plain flour
1 teaspoon baking powder
½ teaspoon bicarbonate of soda
1 teaspoon ground mixed spice
pinch of salt
100g soft unsalted butter
160g dark brown sugar
2 large eggs
3 tablespoons sour cream

125ml boiling water
75g dark chocolate, broken into pieces
1 teaspoon instant coffee
250g instant royal icing
1 packet green ready-to-roll icing
about 30 cranberries for decoration
small holly-leaf cutter with veining stamp
12-bun muffin tin and papers

Preheat the oven to 200°C/gas mark 6.

In a large bowl, mix together the flour, baking powder, bicarb, mixed spice and salt. In another bowl, cream the butter and sugar with an electric mixer. Add the eggs one at a time, mixing well after each addition, and then beat in a third of the flour mixture followed by a tablespoon of the sour cream, repeating till all is used up.

Put the water, chocolate and instant coffee in a pan and heat gently, just until the chocolate's melted. Fold this into the cake batter, but don't overbeat. The mixture will be very thin, but don't worry about that: just pour carefully into the waiting muffin cases and put in the oven for about 20 minutes, until each little cake is cooked through but still dense and damp. Let cool in the tin for 5 minutes, then slip out the cakes in their papers and sit on a wire rack until completely cold.

To ice them, make up the royal icing according to the packet instructions and cover the tops of the cupcakes thickly. Cut out holly leaves and sit two on each cake, and then press on your berries, perhaps putting two on some, three on others.

Makes 12.

BAKLAVA

Of course, I don't really think this is a part of the traditional Yuletide feast, but there is something about the intense sweetness and aromatic succulence that makes it appropriate. It is so temple-achingly sweet that one small marked-out diamond, or maybe two, is enough. But even so, I love its perfumed sugariness – as much as I love the tender, rose-shot green of its equally fragrant nubbly interior. It's also a very good present to take to people over Christmas, which is why I've indicated one of those foil baking trays below.

for the syrup:

300ml water

500g caster sugar

juice of ¹/2 a lemon

1 tablespoon rosewater

1 tablespoon orange-flower water

for the pastry:

325g pistachios, chopped in a
processor until medium–fine

125g unsalted butter, melted

400g (2 packets) filo pastry

square foil tin, 23 x 23 x 4cm from a
supermarket or kitchen shop

To make the syrup: bring the water, sugar and lemon juice to the boil, and keep it at boiling point for 5 minutes. Add the rosewater and flower water, and then remove it from the heat. Pour it into a jug, let it cool and then chill it in the fridge.

Preheat the oven to 180°C/gas mark 4.

Brush the tin with butter, and then each of the filo pastry sheets as you line the tin with them. Use one packet for the bottom layer, placing them in the tin evenly so that the pastry goes up the sides with a little overhang. As the tin is square and the filo pastry is often a rectangular shape, you should try to arrange the sheets so that each side is covered in turn. When you have used one packet, spread the pistachios evenly over the filo sheets. Then carry on with the rest of the pastry in the same way. The last sheet on top should also be buttered well, and then with a sharp knife trim around the top edge of the tin to give a neat finish. Cut parallel lines 4–5cm apart to form diamond shapes, making sure you cut the baklava right through to the bottom of the tin.

Put in the oven and cook for 30 minutes, by which time the filo will have puffed up and become golden-brown. As soon as it comes out of the oven, pour over half the cold syrup. Leave it a few minutes to soak in and then pour over the rest.

Makes approximately 16 pieces.

GAME PIE

The idea of making a raised-crust pie is a daunting one, I know, but I should tell you that a 15-year-old boy, Nick Blake, came to spend a day with us during the photo-shoot for this book, and ended up making the one that you see opposite, without any earlier preparation or experience. These things, you see, are worth attempting. And the beautiful, designed-for-the-purpose tins that you can buy from most kitchen shops take a lot of the uncertainty out of it.

I love grouse so much that it's the only game I want in my pie, but venison, pheasant, wild rabbit, anything you want to use, is fine. I buy fresh veal stock, made by Joubère and available from some butchers, delicatessens and supermarkets.

for the filling:
200g pork belly
150g lean pork
150g lean veal
125g thin rashers of streaky bacon
3 tablespoons Marsala
1 teaspoon English mustard powder
1 teaspoon all-spice
breasts from a brace of grouse or 200g of whatever game you're using

for the pastry:
200ml water

175g lard
500g plain flour
1/2 teaspoon salt
1 large egg, beaten with 1/2 teaspoon salt, to glaze
1 game-pie mould, 22cm long

for the jellied stock:
2 leaves gelatine
225ml veal stock
75ml Marsala
squeeze of lemon
1 teaspoon salt
fresh-ground pepper

Put the pork, veal, bacon, Marsala, a teaspoon of salt, a fair bit of pepper, mustard and the all-spice into the food processor and blitz to a coarse purée, then transfer to a bowl and sit, covered, in the fridge. Chop whatever game you're using into rough chunks and set these aside, too, while you make the pastry.

In a saucepan, bring the water and lard to a boil. Then turn into a bowl containing the flour and salt. Mix everything well, creating a smooth dough. Cover the dough and leave it until it's no longer too hot to handle, but don't let it get cold. Now preheat the oven to 200°C/gas mark 6.

Cut off a quarter of the pastry for the lid, and set it aside, covered, for a while. Using the rest of the pastry, line your beautiful, hinged game-pie mould. Push the pastry up the sides of the tin – gently, though, and making sure there are no cracks. Pack the processed filling into the pastry, adding the rough chunks of game as you go, filling right

CRANBERRY UPSIDE-DOWN CAKE

It's very useful around this time of year to have one or two seasonal puddings to boost a lunch or dinner otherwise made up of leftovers. Not that I wish to imply that leftovers constitute inadequate eating; indeed, it's my favourite sort of food.

I love the Christmasiness of this, all that glowing, berried redness.

50g plus 125g unsalted butter
150g plus 125g caster sugar
175g cranberries
125g self-raising flour
pinch of salt

1 teaspoon cinnamon
2 large eggs
1–1 1/2 tablespoons full-fat milk
tarte-tatin dish, cast-iron straight-sided
20cm frying pan or similar

Preheat the oven to 180°C/gas mark 4, and put in a baking sheet to heat up at the same time.

Put the cast-iron frying pan – or tarte-tatin dish if you've got one – on the hob over a medium heat and melt the 50g of butter. Add the 150g of sugar, stir, then empty in the cranberries and turn to coat in the syrupy liquid. Set aside while you get on with the cake.

Put the flour, salt, cinnamon, 125g of sugar, 125g of butter and the eggs in the processor and blitz to combine. Pulse while you add enough milk down the funnel to make a batter of a soft, dropping consistency. Pour it over the berries in the pan and transfer immediately to the heated baking sheet in the oven. Cook for 30 minutes or until the cake is bouncy, gold and risen, and beginning to shrink back from the edges.

Take out of the oven and place a plate on top of the pan. Turn upside-down and lift the pan off. Be careful here – it's easy to burn yourself, as I prove time and time again.

Serve warm with crème fraîche or ice cream.

Serves 6.

CHRISTMAS CRÈME BRÛLÉE

I don't need to tell you how beautiful this is: you can see. It's extravagant, certainly, but it's meant to be. And it feels like a treat, breaking through that gilt-tortoiseshell crust to the voluptuous depths of egg-nog-scented cream beneath.

The tip of freezing the bowl before pouring in the smooth cream-custard I culled from Simon Hopkinson, for which and for whom I am always grateful.

600ml double cream
1 teaspoon orange-flower water
good grating fresh nutmeg
8 large egg yolks
3 tablespoons caster sugar

6 tablespoons demerara sugar
3–4 sheets edible gold leaf, optional
pie dish approximately 20cm in
   diameter
chef's blowtorch

Put the pie dish in the freezer for at least 20 minutes and half-fill the sink with cold water. Put the cream, orange-flower water and a brave grating of fresh nutmeg into a saucepan, and bring to boiling point, but do not let boil. Beat the egg yolks and caster sugar together in a bowl, and pour the flavoured cream over, still beating. Rinse and dry the pan and pour the custard mix back in. Cook over a medium heat (or low, if you're worried) until the custard thickens: about 10 minutes should do it. You do want this to be a good, voluptuous crème, so don't err on the side of runny caution. Remember you've got your sinkful of cold water to plunge the pan into should it really look as if it's about to split.

When the cream's thick enough, grate over a little more nutmeg and pour into the severely chilled pie dish. Leave to cool, then put in the fridge till truly cold. Sprinkle with demerara sugar, spoonful by spoonful, and burn with a blowtorch till you have a blistered, tortoiseshell carapace on top. Dab edible gold leaf onto the hard but sticky burnt-sugar crust, using a fat pastry brush or, easier still, your fingertips. Press it gently onto the surface in a random but decorative way, smoothing it down.

Serves 8.

BREAD AND YEAST

BREAD AND YEAST

Baking with yeast is the most addictive of pastimes. Once you start, you realize, first, how easy it is, and second, how almost ridiculously satisfying. Partly, this is to do with the feel, the way you sense the dough coming alive under your hands. But perhaps that's what seems spooky to some people – the thought of live yeast. That's why I am such a champion of those little sachets of easy-blend yeast: real, live, fresh yeast isn't hard to use (see below) but the sachet stuff seems more approachable at first.

The point is to get stuck in, and then you can move on to fresh yeast if it's available – and now that most supermarkets have in-store bakeries it tends to be. But if I'm entirely honest, I'm not sure I could detect the difference between bread that's been risen with fresh yeast and bread that's been made with the easy-blend sachets.

The one sort of yeast I cannot, however, get on with is active dried yeast, which manufacturers of bread machines seem so keen on. To me, it tastes too intensely yeasty. And while we're here, I should say that the bread machine leaves me cold, also. Why make bread – when anyway you can buy such wonderful loaves now – if it involves no collaboration on your part? There's none of that crucial satisfaction, that warm feeling of homespun achievement. I don't want to suggest that bread-baking is the province of the terminally smug – the rewards are real, and stem from real activity – but it's very hard not to feel better after kneading dough. As Margaret Costa wrote in her seminal *Four Seasons Cookbook*, it does make 'the baker see herself in an almost biblical light as a valiant woman whose children shall rise up and call her blessed'.

It's also the case that although the bread machine does a good job of kneading the dough it does a pretty hopeless one of baking the loaf. You may disagree, but this has been my experience, and I did once spend some weeks trying one out. And when my experimental time was up, I was very, very glad to send it back.

The baking of the loaf can be a problem: domestic ovens just aren't good at producing that perfect crackly crustiness. You can try all those tricks that are meant to turn your oven into a professional baker's one – spraying the oven with water from a spritzer as you put the loaf in and regularly thereafter, slipping in underneath it a baking tray filled with ice cubes, and so on – but I have never found they work; or not enough to make the faffing about worthwhile.

But still I bake bread, and urge you to. And you can bake good bread, or I wouldn't be telling you about it. For one thing, you can concentrate on loaves which don't rely on a crackly crust; I love white bread baked with just a dusting of flour. The Finnish loaf, too, has a chewy crust, made by glazing it with melted butter the minute it comes out of the oven. True, my sourdough bread may not be quite as the San Franciscans would make it, but it's still tangy, chewy and distinctive. I don't believe even an extremely well-appointed steam-injected oven could improve on them.

I've mentioned the kneading process earlier, and I want to return to it, just in case I've given the impression that I'm entirely of the no-pain-no-gain school: I'm not. There is a very good case for letting a mixer fitted with a dough hook do a lot of the hard work for you. But all I'd say is allow yourself just to finish it off, to do a couple of minutes' therapeutic kneading after the machine's done its efficient business. I think, probably wrongly, that the bread's better for it; certainly I feel better.

My way of baking bread is designed to make it fit more easily into the sort of lives we lead. It can be very hard to find time to leave the dough to rise for a couple of hours, and then another hour, and then bake it. What I do – and it does happen to develop and enrich the taste at the same time – is let the bread rise overnight in a cold place, even the fridge. This means that you can ease yourself out of the day with a little bit of bedtime kneading, and then the next morning all you need to do is let the chilly dough get to room temperature, form it into a loaf or fit it into a tin and then leave it to get puffy and oven-ready while you get dressed or read the papers or whatever. It still means that this is more likely to be undertaken as a weekend or holiday activity, but not exclusively so.

In the recipes that follow, I specify an amount of instant yeast – i.e., yeast that doesn't need to be reconstituted: I do not, ever, mean the extra-fast-acting one – and give as an alternative double the amount of fresh yeast, and then proceed to give, unfamiliarly, exactly the same methods for using both. This is because – as I learnt from a professional baker – you do not need to mix fresh yeast with liquid and then wait for it to foam; you just add it to the flour and so on as if it were the instant sort. I find cutting out this step really does erode any psychological barrier to bread-making.

The quality of flour you use makes a difference. I tend to use organic bread flours from reputable mills, but not exclusively. Don't let lack of time for right-on sourcing be the excuse to stop you from immersing yourself pleasurably – if tentatively at first – in this chapter.

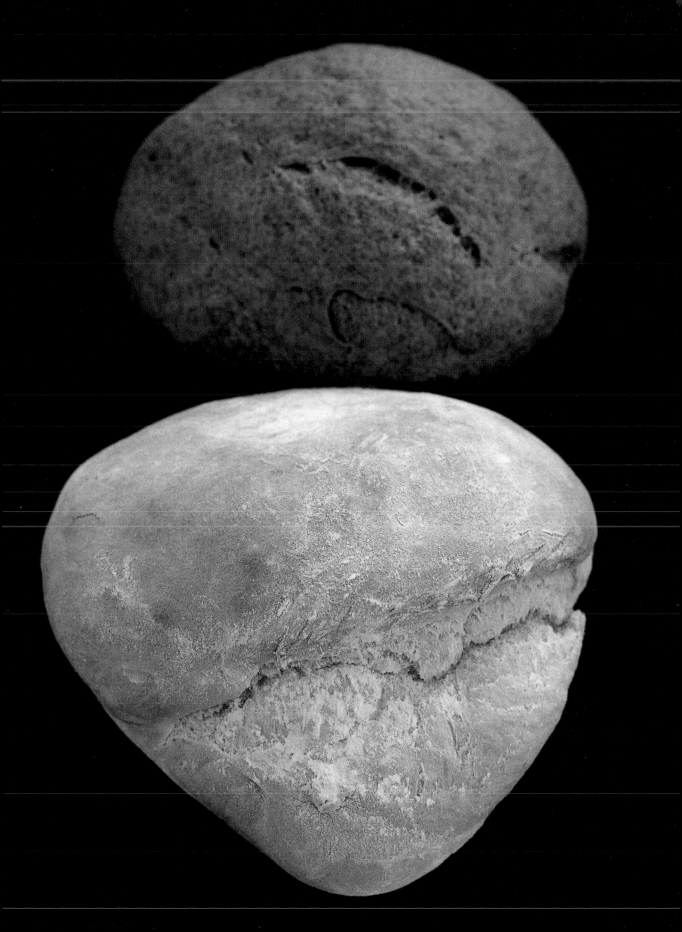

THE ESSENTIAL WHITE LOAF

I love home-made white bread, springy and tender-crumbed, with a crust dusted with oven-caramelized flour. The best tip I can give you for making good white bread with a light crumb that lasts longer before going stale – which is ever the problem with home-made bread – is to plead with you to use old potato water as the liquid. By this, I just mean the water in which peeled potatoes have cooked. Remember, though, to check the saltiness of the water before throwing in the full amount of salt specified below. I am eccentric enough to keep the water when I drain potatoes, and then bag it up in 300ml quantities and stash them in the deep freeze to use when the bread-making urge is next upon me. Otherwise – and this works remarkably well – you can add a scant tablespoonful of instant mash to ordinary warm water. I think it's worth doing this, and not hard to make sure you've got a packet of Smash or whatever in the house, however offensive it might be to your culinary self-image.

Perhaps here is the place to try and impress upon you that all bread recipes are approximate guides; the amount of liquid that flour absorbs changes according to the flour and the weather.

500g strong white bread flour, plus more for kneading

7g (1 sachet) easy-blend yeast or 15g fresh yeast

1 tablespoon salt

approximately 300ml warm tap or potato water

1 tablespoon unsalted butter, softened

1 baking sheet or 500g loaf tin

Put the flour, yeast and salt in a bowl and pour in 200ml of the water, mixing as you do so with a wooden spoon or your hands. Be prepared to add more water, but bear in mind that you want to end up with a shaggy mess (and this of course is the technical term). Add the butter, and mix that in. Now, either start kneading, or if you've got a free-standing mixer, put in the dough hook and let it do the work. Kneading is easy to do but hard to describe. Basically, what you do is press the heel of your hand into the dough, push the dough away, and bring it back and down against the worksurface, for at least 10 minutes. You may need to add more flour as you do so; if the dough seems stickily wet, it means you do want a little more and often a lot more. When you've kneaded enough you will be able to tell the difference – it suddenly feels smoother and less sticky. It's a wonderful moment.

Form the dough into a ball and put into a large oiled or buttered bowl, turning once so the top of the dough is greased. (Most often, I wash out the bowl I've just been using, dry it up and use it again, letting its residual warmth give a starting oomph to the yeast.) Cover with clingfilm and put into a cold place or the fridge overnight, or in a warm place for an hour or two. If you're giving the bread a short warm rise, then just keep an eye on it; it's ready when it's more or less doubled in size. If you've given it a long cold rise, remove the dough from its cold storage – the next morning, later on that day, whenever – and, if it's doubled in size, punch it down, which means doing exactly what that sounds like: punch it until it deflates; I love doing this. If it doesn't look risen much, leave the bowl out at room temperature for a while (obviously, it's easiest to make bread over the weekend so you have a longer morning) and then proceed as above.

Preheat the oven to 220°C/gas mark 7 and then, after kneading the dough for a scant minute, form it into a round loaf shape (or however you want) and sit it on the baking sheet (or in the loaf tin) covered loosely with clingfilm or a tea towel and leave for half an hour or so until puffy and again almost doubled in size. Just before you put it in the oven, remove the towel or plastic and dust with flour; as I've already said, since you can't get a truly crusty loaf from a domestic oven you might as well go for a different effect to start off with.

Bake for 35 minutes or until cooked through; the way to check is to lift up the loaf or remove it from its tin and knock with your knuckles on the underside: if it makes a hollow noise, it's cooked; if not, put it back in the oven for a few minutes. Even if it's been in a tin, do this bit unmoulded. When ready, remove to a rack and let cool, if you can, before eating.

And look, I know that home-baked breads can look bulging and full of cracks and fissures – mine, for example, and see the photo on p295, look rather like the Venus of Willendorf – but that's fine, that's because they're home-made.

MY BROWN BREAD

Everyone has a way of mixing different flours to make the breads they like, and this is one of my favourites for an everyday but highly flavoured brown loaf. Follow the essential white loaf recipe, only replace the 500g white flour with:

200g rye flour   **200g strong white flour**
200g wholewheat flour

Be prepared to add slightly more water – and here use ordinary, not potato, water – and bake the bread in an oven preheated to 200°C/gas mark 6 for about 45 minutes.

POTATO BREAD

This takes the potato-water idea one stage further: you're actually adding cold, cooked potatoes to the dough. This doesn't make a heavy bread, as you might suppose; the whole deal is that the starch in the potato seems to facilitate the yeast and lighten the loaf. But if this is light, it isn't airy: there is a certain chewiness about it, and an almost waxy softness, which makes it perfect for dunking into the wine-dark juices of a rich meat stew. And the toast it makes is incredible.

300g cold or warm boiled potatoes
700–800g strong white flour
1 tablespoon salt
7g (1 sachet) easy-blend yeast or 15g
    fresh yeast

1 tablespoon Greek yoghurt
300ml tepid potato water

1 baking sheet

Press the potatoes through a ricer into a large bowl – or just mash them once in it – and add 600g of the flour together with the salt and the yeast. Mix together, adding the yoghurt and then the water slowly. (Even if your potato water's salty, still add the salt to the flour earlier; on cooking, the potatoes themselves tend to neutralize salinity so you have to emphasize it – though not exaggerate it – at this stage.) When you've got some-thing approaching a dough, tip it out onto a floured surface (or keep it in the bowl and use the mixer's dough hook) and begin kneading, adding more flour as you need it. I find I can end up using another 200g or so.

This is damper and stickier than ordinary white bread dough, so be prepared to keep kneading for a bit longer, but when you have something that looks like it's hanging together densely (I give it about 10 minutes in my KitchenAid with the dough hook fitted, then 2 minutes by hand), form a heavy ball – it won't be very neat – put it into a buttered bowl, turn to coat well, cover with clingfilm and leave in a cold place overnight or a warm place for an hour or so.

When the dough's doubled in size, punch it down, letting any repressed anger joyfully out, knead for a minute and form into a loaf of whatever shape pleases you, and preheat the oven to 220°C/gas mark 7. Sit it on the baking sheet, loosely covered with a tea towel, and after about 30 minutes, when the bread's puffy and almost doubled in size, put it in the oven for 20 minutes, before turning the temperature down to 190°C/gas mark 5 and giving it another 10 minutes or until it's cooked through. Test, as usual, by knocking on the loaf's underside: when cooked, it should give a distinctly hollow sound.

Remove from the oven and let cool on a rack.

FINNISH RYE BREAD

This is my adaptation of a wonderful loaf which comes from the equally wonderful Beatrice Ojakangas. It's dense, dark and aromatic in an extraordinarily comforting way. I'm not Finnish, and yet I warm to this loaf as if I were brought up on it.

225g rye flour
300g strong white flour
7g (1 sachet) easy-blend yeast or
   15g fresh yeast
1 tablespoon dark muscovado sugar

2 teaspoons salt
300ml warm water
45g (3 tablespoons) unsalted butter,
   melted
1 baking sheet

Put the flours, yeast, sugar and salt into a large bowl and slowly add the water, mixing with your hands or a wooden spoon, until you've got a messy but vaguely cohesive lump of dough. Add a tablespoonful of the melted butter and mix just to incorporate it. Start kneading, either by hand or with the dough hook, until the dough comes together smoothly to form a dense ball, adding more water or flour (and I use the strong white, not the rye, mainly) as necessary.

Use some more of the melted butter to grease a bowl and turn the dough ball in it so that the top is oily (and won't therefore dry out), then cover the bowl with clingfilm and leave to rise in a cold place overnight or for an hour or so somewhere warm.

When the dough's doubled in size, punch it down. This is never quite as satisfying with dense doughs as it is with white breads, but it's pleasurable all the same. Give a good few kneads, and then form into a round loaf. Sit the loaf on the baking sheet, cover it with a tea towel and leave to get puffy for about 30 minutes, during which time preheat the oven to 190°C/gas mark 5. Bake for 45–55 minutes, or until the loaf is cooked through. It should sound hollow when you rap it on its underside with your knuckles, and an inserted skewer should come out clean.

Brush with the remaining tablespoon of melted butter and leave on a wire rack to cool.

SOURDOUGH

The reason this isn't quite a real sourdough is that it uses a teeny-weeny bit of yeast in the starter, rather than relying only on wild yeasts picked up from the atmosphere. I am not going to give an entire history and account of what a sourdough loaf is, but it helps to think of it as a bread made in three parts, with time in between for the dough to mature and acquire the characteristic tang. I know the idea of a long-drawn-out, tripartite baking process is not necessarily a welcome one, but presumably you do this because you want to, not because you are trying to find time-saving ways in the kitchen and kind of stumbled onto this by mistake.

Anyway, first you have the starter, which is really just a mixture of flour and water, with – and this is the unorthodox, not to say improper, way I do it – the addition of a drop of milk and pinch of yeast. You leave this to get good and sour and bubbly, and then you use some of it to mix the second part – the sponge – with more flour and water. Third and finally, you make the dough, which is the sponge with, again, more flour and more water. I add yeast to this; I'm not sure I should, but the American who first showed me the way of the sourdough did, so I carry on in this vein.

It is the method which is significant with sourdough; you can decide which flours you use to make it. I tend to make rye sourdough or an ordinary white sourdough loaf. I say ordinary, but it isn't at all. It's rather like – and is indeed related to – that wonderful, dense and chewy French *pain gris*. And I've made good bread by using the rye starter in a loaf otherwise made exclusively with white flour too.

The hardest thing about sourdough is not making the bread but keeping the starter alive. I always forget to feed it, which is the term used for adding flour and water to it regularly to keep it going. It dies on me. Or rather, I should say, I kill it out of neglect. To keep it alive, every time you use a cup, stir in another ½ cup of water and ¾ cup of flour and leave out of the fridge for 4 hours. Do this once a fortnight if you can.

for the starter:
150g rye or strong white flour
pinch of yeast from an easy-blend
yeast sachet (like a small pinch of
salt) or a fatter pinch of fresh yeast

½ teaspoon of milk
approximately 200ml water

Combine the flour, yeast and milk and as much water to make a mixture like a thick pancake batter, and leave, loosely covered, for 3 days.

for the sponge:

180ml of starter

180ml of warm water

100g rye or strong white flour

If you've got American cup measures, you can use the ³/₄-cup measure for this, which is roughly the equivalent of 180ml. It makes measuring out very much easier.

Mix all the ingredients together and leave tightly covered for 12–18 hours; longer is better but the shorter time is enough if that's all you've got.

for the dough:

375g wholemeal bread flour (for the rye sourdough) or 500g strong white flour

the rest of the easy-blend yeast sachet or 15g fresh yeast

all the of the sponge from above

1 scant tablespoon salt

1 tablespoon caraway seeds (for rye sourdough only)

250–300ml warm water

vegetable oil for greasing bowl

1 baking sheet

Put the flour and yeast in a large bowl, then stir in the other ingredients till you've got a shaggy mess that looks like it's on its way to becoming a dough. Knead, either by hand or by machine, adding more flour as needed, to form a dense, smooth dough.

Form into a ball and put in an oiled bowl, turning once so that the top is also greased. Cover with clingfilm and leave to double in size, either overnight in a cold place or the fridge, or for an hour or so somewhere warm.

When the dough's done its stuff, punch it down, knead it for 1–2 minutes and form it into a round loaf and sit it, covered with a tea towel, on a baking sheet. Preheat the oven to 200°C/gas mark 6, and let the oven warm up while the loaf is left, for about 30 minutes, until it's puffy.

Uncover, and score the top of the loaf. For ease, you should use a razor blade or *lame* for this, but a sharp knife will do. It must be very sharp, though, because you don't want to use any pressure or the now nicely puffy loaf will deflate. I make about 5 slashes all the way over the top diagonally one way, and then the other to make a rough chequerboard design. Transfer to the oven and bake for about 45 minutes, until the loaf is cooked and sounds hollow when you rap it firmly on its underside.

NORWEGIAN MOUNTAIN LOAF

This was one of the recipes – along with the cinnamon buns on p322 – I greedily plundered from Trine Bell, a friend who's half Norwegian and is generous with her culinary birthright. As much as I love a good, British white loaf, I have a real weakness for those nubbly Northern European breads which are dense and virtuously substantial.

Because this is very easy to make, it can soon become part of a pretty painless routine. You can play around, as you like, with flours, seeds and grains.

250ml semi-skimmed milk
250ml water
350g wholemeal bread flour
50g rye flour
7g (1 sachet) easy-blend yeast or
   15g fresh yeast
50g porridge oats (not instant)

25g wheatgerm
3 tablespoons sunflower seeds
3 tablespoons linseeds
1 tablespoon salt
silicon loaf-shaped mould or baking
   sheet or ordinary well-buttered
   loaf tin

Mix the milk and water together in a measuring jug, and combine all the other ingredients in a large bowl. Pour the liquid into the dry ingredients, stirring all the while, to make a sticky, porridge-like mixture.

Scrape into an incredibly well-buttered loaf tin – or better still, a Paton Calvert silicon loaf mould which you need not prepare in any way – and put into a cold oven. Turn it on to 110°C/gas mark ¼ and after 30 minutes turn it up to 180°C/gas mark 4. Bake for 1 hour, though in some ovens it may need 10–15 minutes more. You should be able to slip it out of its tin and check by the knocking method, but with a loaf of this heaviness that's not always a reliable gauge, so do poke in a cake-tester or fine skewer to make sure; if it comes out clean, the loaf's cooked. If not, you can just put it back into the oven without its tin and give it another few minutes.

MAPLE-PECAN BREAD

You won't find much in the way of flavoured breads here, fashionable though they are. I don't go in for them. Bread, like a pasta, is best at conveying other flavours, not jumping about in a ra-ra skirt showing off its own. But this is an exception: it has nuts and syrup in, but the overall effect is muted. And it stays true to its proper calling: that's to say, this is a bread that comes into its own with cheese.

500g wholemeal bread flour
150g strong white flour
1 tablespoon salt
7g (1 sachet) easy-blend yeast or
15g fresh yeast
300–400ml warm water

4 tablespoons maple syrup
50–100g chopped pecans (or walnuts)
oil (walnut oil, if you've got some) or
butter for greasing
1 baking sheet

Combine the flours, salt and yeast in a large bowl. Measure out 300ml of the warm water and stir in the maple syrup. Pour the liquid into the dry ingredients and stop when you've got a rough dough; you may need an extra 100ml or so of water to reach this stage. Knead for a few minutes, then leave for 20 minutes.

Start kneading again, sprinkling in the nuts. It's entirely up to you how nutty to make this: with cheese I think the upper limit is fine; as an ordinary eating loaf, I'd go for the lighter amount. Carry on kneading until the dough feels smooth and elastic (though this amount of wholemeal means it can't feel that elastic) and then form into a ball.

Grease a bowl with oil, and turn the dough ball in the oil, so that the top is lightly slicked with it too. Cover the bowl with clingfilm and leave to rise in the kitchen for 1–2 hours or until about doubled, or follow the general method for a cold, slow rise.

Punch the dough down, knead for 1 minute and then form into a loaf. Sit this loaf on a baking sheet, cover with a tea towel, preheat the oven to 220°C/gas mark 7 and leave the dough for about 30 minutes or until puffy.

Score the loaf with a blade or sharp knife – I tend just to give three short diagonal slashes on this one – and transfer to the oven. After 15 minutes, turn the temperature down to 190°C/gas mark 5 and give a further 20 minutes or so. Check the bread's ready by rapping its bottom, then transfer to a wire rack to cool.

BAGELS

I know that making your own bagels seems like a fairly abstruse practice. I include a recipe partly because most of the bagels for sale here are not bagels at all, but bread rolls with a hole in the middle – real bagels should be chewy, not remotely airy, with a tightly woven crumb – but also because they're a pleasure to make. They belong here, and not in the children's chapter, though children really enjoy making them, or rather forming them. I do too.

The cooking isn't hard – though it's a dough that needs muscle power – even if it is a two-staged affair: you poach them first, and then bake them. The recipe is adapted from George Greenstein's *Secrets of a Jewish Baker* – where else should you be getting a bagel recipe? – whose tip it is to add malt to the poaching liquid to help the bagels acquire that characteristic sweet and shiny crust. Malt syrup, or extract, is sold at most chemists; but failing that, just use sugar.

1kg strong white flour, plus more as necessary for kneading

1 tablespoon salt

7g (1 sachet) easy-blend yeast or 15g fresh yeast

2 tablespoons sugar

1 tablespoon vegetable oil, plus more for greasing

500ml warm water, plus more as needed

2 tablespoons malt or sugar, for poaching the bagels

2–3 baking sheets, oiled or greased

Combine the flour, salt and yeast together in a large bowl. Add the sugar and oil to the water. Make a well in the dry ingredients and add the liquid, mixing to a dough with a spatula or wooden spoon.

Knead the dough either by hand or with a dough hook, trying to add more flour if you can. Often with doughs you want them as wet as you can manage; here, dry is good.

The dough will be very stiff and hard work, I know, but knead until you've got a really smooth, elastic dough; even with the dough hook and an electric mixer, this takes about 10 minutes.

Form the dough into a ball, and put it into an oiled bowl, turning once to coat all round, then cover the bowl with clingfilm and leave it to rise for about 1 hour. It should be well risen, and, when you poke it with your finger, the impression should remain.

Now punch the dough down, really punch, and then give a good knead and divide the dough into 3 pieces. Using your hands, roll each piece into a rope, then cut each rope into 5 pieces. Roll each piece between the palms of your hands into a ball, and

then roll into another rope, curling it round to form a ring. Seal the ends by overlapping them a little and pinching them together. At about this time put on a large pan of water to boil. When it boils, add the malt or sugar.

Sit the bagels on the baking sheets, cover with tea towels and leave for about 20 minutes, by which time they should be puffy. Now preheat the oven to 240°C/gas mark 9 or your maximum oven temperature.

When the malted water's boiling and your bagels are good and puffy, start poaching them. Drop a couple of bagels at a time into the boiling water and boil for 1 minute, turning them once. I use a couple of large spatulas for this (wasn't it Portnoy who always presumed spatula was a Yiddish word?).

As you poach them, put them back onto the oiled baking sheets, well spaced, then bake for 10–15 minutes or until they're shiny and golden-brown.

Makes 15 bagels.

GARLIC AND PARSLEY HEARTHBREADS

These are something between garlic nan and herby focaccia: dimpled, doughy and headily pungent. When lunch is cold and sparse – some sharp cheese, some sliced tomatoes, a green salad – these bring everything substantially, chin-drippingly together. (But please try making them once to eat with fried eggs and maybe some fried or grilled tomatoes.)

500g strong white flour
7g (1 sachet) instant yeast or
** 15g fresh yeast**
1 tablespoon salt
300–400ml warm water
5 tablespoons olive oil, plus more for
** greasing and for pouring over the**
** garlic**

3 large or 4 small heads of garlic
extra virgin olive oil for drizzling
bunch of flat-leaf parsley
salt, preferably Maldon, for sprinkling
2 baking sheets

Preheat the oven to 190°C/gas mark 5.

Combine the flour, yeast and salt in a bowl. Pour 300ml warm water into a measuring jug and stir in the olive oil. Mix the liquid with the dry ingredients to make a soft but firm dough, adding more liquid as needed, and either turn this out onto a surface and knead by hand or keep in the bowl and use a mixer fitted with the dough hook and knead until smooth, supple and full of elastic life. Form into a ball, wash out

NIGELLAN FLATBREAD

Look, the name is meant to be a bit of joke, but what I'm talking about is a pitta-like bread, glazed golden with beaten egg and sprinkled with nigella seeds. I came across a recipe rather like it in Eric Treuille and Ursula Ferrigno's inspirational *Bread* and made it, you could say, my own. (You can get the nigella seeds, usually marked 'kalonji', from shops that sell Indian food, and many more besides.)

This is what I make when I'm in mezze-mode. It's not hard, and although I love some of the flatbreads you can buy (not particularly the pittas, but the doughier, softer, tear-shaped hearthbreads), it gives me more pleasure to make these, doubling the quantity and putting the flat oval loaves in the oven in batches so there's always a wooden board of warm, dippable bread on the table.

for the bread:

500g strong white bread flour

7g (1 sachet) easy-blend yeast or
  15g fresh yeast

2 teaspoons salt

2 tablespoons yoghurt

2 tablespoons olive oil, plus more for
  greasing

approximately 300ml warm water

for the glaze:

1 large egg

1 teaspoon water

1 teaspoon yoghurt

1 tablespoon nigella seeds

2 baking sheets

Combine the flour, yeast and salt in a large bowl and make a well. Dollop the yoghurt and oil into a measuring jug and add warm water to come up to the 350ml mark. Give a quick beat with a fork to combine, then pour this liquid into the dry ingredients, and mix with your hands or a wooden spoon, adding more liquid as needed, to form a firm but soft dough.

Turn out onto a floured surface (or set your mixer and dough hook to work) and start kneading. Add more flour as needed until you've got a smooth, supple and elastic dough. Form the dough into a ball, grease a bowl and turn the dough in it so it's lightly oiled all over. Cover the bowl with clingfilm and leave to rise for about an hour or so, until doubled in size.

Punch the dough down, then leave to rest for 10 minutes. Preheat the oven to 220°C/gas mark 7. Tear the dough into 3, and then halve each piece. Form each of these 6 little pieces into an egg-shape and, one by one, roll them out to make a flat, elongated, if irregular oval. Place on baking sheets about 3cm apart, cover with tea towels and leave to prove for 20 minutes, until puffy.

Using the blunt side of an ordinary kitchen knife, draw diagonal parallel lines

PIZZA CASARECCIA

This is the pizza as made in the Calabrian home of my own domestic goddess, Lisa Grillo. While we all struggle to produce that thin-crusted, charcoal-redolent pizzaiolo's pizza and fail, the Italians recognize that you need to go to the pizzeria for that and have instead devised a home-made alternative, doughier and with more topping, but very good in its own but different way.

I've marked the anchovies for the topping as optional, but in truth all of it is. The list that follows was how Lisa made it, but I suspect it was how Lisa made it because that was what she had in the house. And as for the cheese, don't worry if you don't have parmesan or mozzarella: Italians are mad about Cheddar on pizza.

for the dough:
250g plain flour, preferably Italian 00
1 heaped teaspoon (1/2 sachet)
  easy-blend dried yeast, or 3
  tablespoons fresh
1/2 teaspoon salt
approximately 150ml warm water
2 tablespoons extra virgin olive oil
1 baking sheet

for the topping:
200g tinned chopped tomatoes
2–3 pinches dried oregano
4 slices fine-cut ham
2–3 gherkins, chopped
5 anchovies, optional
fresh parmesan, mozzarella or cheese
  of your choice

Combine the flour, yeast and salt in a large bowl, and stir in the warm water and the olive oil, adding more water as necessary to form a dough. When you've got a shaggy mess that's on its way to being a dough, tip the contents out onto a lightly floured surface and knead for about 5 minutes (or do all this with an electric mixer's dough hook) or until the dough is smooth and bouncy, though expect this still to be on the sticky side. Put into an oiled bowl and turn it to cover it lightly with the oil. Then cover the bowl with cling-film and leave somewhere warm for an hour till the dough's doubled in size.

Preheat the oven 240°C/gas mark 9.

Knock the air out of the dough using well-oiled hands, knead a little, and press onto the baking sheet in either a rectangular or round shape. Cover with the chopped tomatoes which have been seasoned with some salt, pepper and the oregano. Put into the very hot oven for about 20 minutes or until the dough has a hollow sound when knocked.

Add the topping of your choice, then put the pizza back in the oven and cook for a further 5–10 minutes or until the cheese has melted and the base is crisp.

Serves 4 generously.

GERMAN PLUM TART

I first made this a couple of years ago now, and it was one of the recipes that drew me to yeast cookery, made me want to do more. The inspirational force is Linda Collister – you just cannot read her without wanting to put on an apron and get your hands stuck into some flour – and this comes from *Sweet Pies and Tarts*. While the two yeasted flat tarts that follow this are more suitable for long, greedy weekend breakfasts, this makes a sumptuous pudding. You could easily make the dough in the morning, sit it in the fridge for a slow rise all day and then, with relative lack of effort, get this finished once you've got back from work, even if it's quite late. And the one thing it doesn't taste like is a hastily knocked-up little something.

for the dough:
**3¹/₂g (¹/₂ sachet) easy-blend yeast
 or 7g fresh yeast**
about 350g strong white bread flour
¹/₂ teaspoon salt
50g golden caster sugar
200ml milk, lukewarm
1 medium egg, beaten
20g unsalted butter, very soft

for the filling:
500g plums, halved and stoned

3 tablespoons demerara sugar

for the crumble topping:
140g plain flour
100g light muscovado sugar
110g unsalted butter, diced
200g walnut or pecan pieces
**1 large baking sheet – about 32 x
 24cm – greased or non-stick, or a
 roasting tin approximately 20 x 30
 x 5cm, also greased or non-stick**

To make the dough, put the flour, yeast, salt and sugar into a mixing bowl, and slowly pour in the warm milk, stirring as you do so. Add the beaten egg and the soft butter, and stir to a soft and sticky dough. Turn out onto a floured board and knead for a good 10 minutes, or for about half that time in an electric mixer fitted with a dough hook. Don't use a food processor. The dough should be soft and satiny but not stickily wet: if you think you need to add more flour, then do; different flours absorb different amounts of liquid. Cover and let rise for 1 hour at room temperature.

To prepare the filling, toss the prepared plums with the sugar (and I sometimes use half light muscovado, half caster rather than the stipulated demerara) and set aside.

Preheat the oven to 190°C/gas mark 5.

To make the crumble topping, combine the flour with the sugar in a mixing bowl, then work in the butter with your fingers to make pea-sized clumps of dough. Stir in the nuts and set aside.

Knock down the risen dough with your knuckles, and push out into a rectangle to cover the baking sheet or press it out in the roasting tin. (This is easier than rolling it and then transferring it, and you are not trying to produce a smooth, even finish.) Top with the plums, cut side up, then sprinkle with the nutty crumble topping. Bake in the preheated oven for about 30 minutes until the base is golden, the fruit tender and the topping crisp and brown.

Serve warm, with cream, crème fraîche or ice cream – vanilla or Hill Station's cinnamon if you can get it.

Serves 8.

VARIATIONS

You can use whatever fruit you like here, with or without the topping or a version thereof. Cherries, messily stoned over the pastry sheet so that you lose none of the juices, are wonderful, especially with almonds in place of the pecans. Apples are also good, with or without blackberries. The wonderful thing about this yeasted pastry is that it absorbs and acts as a foil to any amount of fruity juiciness.

But please, don't rule out a yeasted base for savoury tarts, too. Sweat onions or leeks in butter or bacon fat and spread them out on a puffy sheet of dough made by following the recipe above, but leaving out the sugar, zest and spices. Grate over cheese if so wished, cut into rough squares and eat while still warm.

APPLE KUCHEN

Kuchen, in German, just means cake. In America, it means something more specific – that yeasted, plain, but often fruit-topped, coffee cake that the German immigrants brought with them to the New World. As you might expect, it is good with coffee, and makes a fabulous breakfast if you've got people staying and you want to sit around the table eating, drinking, talking, reading the papers in an aromatic fug of apple-pie spice and buttery yeasty dough.

What I do is make the dough up before I go to bed and leave it, clingfilmed, etc., in the fridge overnight. When I get up the next morning, I turn on the oven, let the dough come back to room temperature and then I get on with the rest. It's probably ready about an hour after I've got up which, considering how spectacular this is, is not bad going. It freezes well, too, so you can always do one batch to last you over a few weekends' worth of breakfasts.

for the dough:

350–400g strong white flour

1/2 teaspoon salt

50g caster sugar

3 1/2g (1/2 sachet) easy-blend yeast, or 7g fresh yeast

2 large eggs

1/2 teaspoon vanilla extract

grated zest of 1/2 a lemon

good grating fresh nutmeg

125ml milk, lukewarm

50g unsalted butter, softened

Swiss-roll tin or ovenproof rectangular dish approximately 30 x 20cm

for the topping:

1 large egg

1 tablespoon of cream

grating of fresh nutmeg

2 Granny Smiths

1 tablespoon demerara sugar

1 tablespoon caster sugar

1/4 teaspoon allspice

2 tablespoons flaked almonds

for the icing:

75g unrefined (golden) icing sugar, sieved

1 tablespoon hot water

Put 350g of the flour in a bowl with the salt, sugar and yeast. Beat the eggs and add them, with the vanilla, lemon zest and nutmeg, to the lukewarm milk. Stir the liquid ingredients into the dry ingredients, to make a medium-soft dough, being prepared to add more flour as necessary. I generally use about 400g, but advise you to start off with the smaller amount: just add more as needed. Work in the soft butter and knead by hand for about 10 minutes or half that time by machine. When the dough is ready it will appear smoother, and springier. It suddenly seems to plump up into glossy life.

Cover with a teatowel and leave till doubled (1–1 1/4 hours), or leave to rise slowly in a cold place overnight. Then punch down and press to line the tin. You may

NORWEGIAN CINNAMON BUNS

The Northern Europeans, and especially the Scandinavians, are wonderful bakers and eating these for breakfast or tea on a cold winter's day makes one feel ours is a climate to be grateful for. But then, I've always thought that bad weather has its compensations, most of them culinary.

for the dough:

600g flour

100g sugar

1/2 teaspoon salt

21g (3 sachets – yes, really) of easy-blend yeast or 45g fresh yeast

100g butter

400ml milk

2 eggs

for the filling:

150g soft, unsalted butter

150g sugar

1 1/2 teaspoons cinnamon

1 egg, beaten, to glaze

roasting tin approximately 33cm x 24cm or large brownie tin, lined with baking parchment bottom and sides

Preheat the oven to 230°C/gas mark 8.

Combine the flour, sugar, salt and yeast in a large bowl. Melt the butter and whisk it into the milk and eggs, then stir it into the flour mixture. Mix to combine and then knead the dough either by hand or using the dough hook of a food mixer until its smooth and springy. Form into a ball, place in an oiled bowl, cover with clingfilm and leave it to rise for about 25 minutes.

Take one-third of the dough and roll it or stretch it to fit your tin; this will form the bottom of each bun when it has cooked. Roll out the rest of the dough on a lightly floured surface, aiming to get a rectangle of roughly 50 x 25cm. Mix the filling ingredients in a small bowl and then spread the rectangle with the buttery cinnamon mixture. Try to get even coverage on the whole of the dough. Roll it up from the longest side until you have a giant sausage. Cut the roll into 2cm slices which should make about 20 rounds. Sit the rounds in lines on top of the dough in the tin, swirly cut-side up. Don't worry if they don't fit snugly together as they will swell and become puffy when they prove. Brush them with egg and then let them rise again for about 15 minutes to let them get duly puffy.

Put in the hot oven and cook for 20–25 minutes, by which time the buns will have risen and will be golden-brown in colour. Don't worry if they catch in places – see mine in the picture. Remove them from the tin and leave to cool slightly on a rack – it's easy just to pick up the whole sheet of parchment and transfer them like that – before letting people tear them off, to eat warm.

Makes 20.

PROCESSOR DANISH PASTRY

I've mentioned Beatrice Ojakangas already in the recipe for Finnish rye bread. I came across her joyfully easy way of making Danish pastry in Dorie Greenspan's *Baking with Julia*. I've adapted it to fit my practice and prejudices, but her idea of mixing everything in the food processor is revolutionary. Truthfully, I don't think I'd even have considered making Danish pastry otherwise. It's good to know, indeed crucial, that this still produces an authentic Danish pastry. Beatrice Ojakangas helpfully writes, 'Don't think you're cheating by taking the fast track – this is the way it's done these days all over Denmark.'

60ml warm water
125ml milk, at room temperature
1 large egg, at room temperature
350g white bread flour
7g (1 sachet) easy-blend yeast or
15g fresh yeast

1 teaspoon salt
25g caster sugar
250g unsalted butter, cold, cut into
1/2cm slices

Pour the water and milk into a measuring jug and add the egg, beating with a fork to mix. Put to one side for a moment. Get out a large bowl, then put the flour, yeast, salt and sugar in the processor, and give one quick whizz just to mix. Add the cold slices of butter and process briefly so that the butter is cut up a little, though you still want visible chunks of at least 1cm. Empty the contents of the food processor into the large bowl and quickly add the contents of the jug. Use your hands or a rubber spatula to fold the ingredients together, but don't overdo it: expect to have a gooey mess with some butter lumps pebbling it. Cover the bowl with clingfilm, put in the fridge and leave overnight or up to 4 days.

To turn it into pastry, take it out of the fridge, let it get to room temperature and roll it out to a 50 x 50cm square. Fold the dough square into thirds, like a business letter, turning it afterwards so that the closed fold is on your left, like the spine of a book. Roll out again to a 50cm square, repeating the steps above 3 times. Since each recipe below uses half of this, cut in half, wrap both pieces and put each in the fridge for 30 minutes (you can keep them in the fridge for up to 4 days, if you haven't already done so at the earlier stage), or refrigerate one to use now and put the other half in the deep freeze to use later.

Having made the Danish pastry, you need to know what to do with it. Obviously, the first stop is to go into making what we call Danish pastries, and they call 'Vienna bread'. There are two here: my all-time favourite, a cheese Danish, which you can rarely buy over here; and an almond Danish, exquisite and much better than even a good shop-bought one.

TARTE TATIN
For Aunt Fel, 1934–2000

Tarte tatin is so overdone that I never thought I'd be including it in any book I wrote. And if tarte tatin is to be undertaken, it isn't, usually, with Danish pastry. But having made this Danish pastry, I knew instantly that it would be perfect in a tarte tatin. So I overruled myself.

I've relied a lot on my Aunt Fel's taste and judgement while working on this book, and indeed while cooking generally, and I invited her round to eat and give her comments on this. She loved it, and insofar as one can dedicate a recipe to someone's memory, I dedicate this to hers.

100g unsalted butter
150g caster sugar
1kg Coxes apples, peeled, quartered
 and cored

half-measure Danish pastry, rolled
 out and ready to use, as above
22cm tarte-tatin dish, similar-shaped
 Le Creuset or cast-iron frying pan

Preheat the oven to 200°C/gas mark 6 and put in a baking sheet at the same time.

Put the butter in the tarte-tatin dish or cast-iron frying pan on the hob. Let the butter melt and add the sugar. When it foams, add the prepared apples, arranging them in a circular pattern, hump-side down, in the dish. Cook on a high heat until the buttery, sugary juices turn a glorious caramel colour and the fruit has softened.

Take the pan off the heat, and leave it to stand for 10 minutes.

Roll the Danish pastry out thinly into a circle to fit the top of the dish, plus a bit of overhang. Lay it on top of the apples in the dish, tucking the edges down the sides under the apples, rather like tucking in a sheet. Transfer the dish to the baking sheet in the oven and cook for 20–30 minutes, until the pastry is golden-brown and the caramel syrup is bubbling.

Take the cooked tarte out of the oven, place a large plate on top of the dish and, wearing oven gloves and with great care, turn the whole thing the other way up. Remove the dish and, *voilà*, your tarte tatin, with its gloriously burnished crown of caramelized fruits. Pick up any apples which have stuck to the dish or that are otherwise out of position, and bring to the table with a small bowl of cold crème fraîche.

Serves 6.

VARIATION
You can also use quinces, either by adding just a few, in among the apples (the most harmonious way, I think), or by substituting them entirely.

THE DOMESTIC GODDESS'S LARDER

THE DOMESTIC GODDESS'S LARDER

There are few things that make us feel so positively domestic as putting food in store. 'Putting up', it always used to be called, the canning and preserving of the fruits and vegetables presently in glut but soon to disappear. Life's not quite like that now, but I do preserve fruits and pickle vegetables for the simple reason that I love doing it. I feel I'm putting down roots, laying down a part of the foundation for living.

But please, I'm not getting into Mrs Bridges drag and don't suggest you do either. I'm not talking about buying bushels and pecks – whatever they may be – of produce and slaving over them for weeks on end. When I make jam, I sometimes make only one small pot at a time. For a start, it's much easier, and I suggest you begin your jam-making career just as sparsely. And few of us anyway have more than a scant shelf on which to store such things. But a few jars here and there are enough to adorn, give pleasure and be useful. It's true that we bought the house we now live in purely because I fell in love with the larder, had to have one, but I recognize that, in cities at any rate, certainly in any modern home, they no longer exist. A cupboard or a few centimetres' space on a counter top or shelf is fine, though. And in fact, many of the foods in this chapter actually need to be stored in the fridge.

I haven't forgotten the modern world; I wanted to concentrate on jams, chutneys, curds and pickles that were easy to make, required no expertise or experience and didn't take days or depend upon multi-staged procedures. I know the idea of being in the kitchen faffing around with bottles and jars and hot pans might seem confining to many, but honestly, I have found it liberating. The sense of connectedness you get, with your kitchen, your home, your food, is the very opposite of constraint. Just follow one suggestion, one recipe in this chapter and I promise you'll see what I mean.

CLEAN JARS

Before you do anything, to store jams, chutneys, glazes, jellies, etc., you need sterilized jars. I have to say, I regard a dishwasher-cleaned jar as a sterilized jar, but you do have to use it straight away, while it's still warm from the machine. Otherwise, you can sterilize the jars in the microwave by filling them a quarter full with water and microwaving them on high for 10 minutes. Drain and use while still warm.

The conventional method for rigorous sterilizing of jars involves scrubbing them well in warm soapy water, rinsing them and then letting them dry off in a cool oven (140°C/gas mark 1). Again, you should put the jam in them while they're still warm, so you may as well leave the jars in the oven until you need them.

VANILLA SUGAR

750g caster sugar   **2 vanilla pods**

Fill a vacuum-sealable glass jar with the caster sugar and the vanilla pods, each cut into 3; after a week you will have sugar infused with the sort of domestically heady fragrance that seems as if it could only have come from the most well-stocked and well-ordered of Victorian larders. It's the aromatic equivalent of well-worn, ambrosially evocative, cream-painted tongue-and-groove panelling.

You can use it in place of ordinary sugar in cakes, pies, puddings – more or less anything sweet. You can even make this your kitchen-counter sugar pot, though have non-scented available for tea drinkers. This is good in coffee, and there's nothing nicer than mugs of vanilla-scented warm milk at bedtime.

VARIATIONS

You can go quite to town with scented sugars. In place of the vanilla pods, use cinnamon sticks, unsprayed rose petals or dried tangerine peel, which you can find in Chinese and most Asian stores. I also keep a store of rosemary sugar, which is just caster sugar with a few sprigs of rosemary – the needles eventually fall off of their own accord – and use, sparsely, to sweeten meat or tomato sauces for pasta and on the rosemary loaf cake on p9.

RHUBARB SCHNAPPS

In the middle of one night, I realized that, however great my love for rhubarb, I had never drunk a liqueur made from it. This, then, is my version. Use the measurements as guidance only. As with the quince brandy below, really it comes down to choosing quantities to fit into whatever jars or bottles you have available.

approximately 1kg of rhubarb, to make 600g trimmed weight
300g caster sugar

1 litre vodka, plus more if needed
1 x 2-litre jar
1 x 1-litre bottle

Chop the rhubarb and divide it between the two jars. Add 150g sugar to each jar, put the lids on and shake well. Unclip the lids and pour 500ml of vodka – and I use the cheapest I can find – into each to fill. If that doesn't fill them, then pour in more. But it should; the rhubarb takes up a lot of each jar.

Close the lids, put the rhubarb somewhere cool and dark for at least 6 weeks and up to 6 months. If you remember, shake the jars every day or every other day for the first month or so.

Strain into a jug, then pour into a bottle. There's your rhubarb schnapps.

Makes 1 litre.

QUINCE BRANDY

To tell the truth I made this partly because I'd bought masses of quinces out of exuberance and excitement because they were in season and then felt increasingly guilty because I'd been too exhausted and busy to do anything with them. So I did this. Of course, now I'll do it every year: it is so peachily delicious. The quinces and the aromatic spices mellow the brandy, and their fragrances hover around just enough to let you know they're there. Use this for the quincemeat, and indeed the Christmas pudding, on pp265 and 256 – and in anything else that you think would benefit from it.

I don't bottle this: I leave it in its beautiful jar, like something you imagine William Morris dreaming of, and use a small, lipped ladle to spoon it out into shot glasses after dinner.

4–6 quinces
approximately 4 bottles cheap
  brandy, or as needed to fill jar

2 large or 4 small cinnamon sticks
4 star anise
1 x 5-litre jar

Wipe your quinces with kitchen towels, then cut and quarter them; but don't peel them or core them. Put them in the bottom of a large, wide-mouthed bottle or jar and pour cheap brandy over to come to the top. Arrange the cinnamon sticks and star anise in this amber underwater scene and fasten the lid. Leave for at least 6 weeks before drinking.

Makes approximately 2 litres.

QUINCE GLAZE

Quince jelly – which is the traditional use to which British quinces are put – seems to me to involve an exhausting and masochistic procedure. Take a tree of quinces, several days' dripping through elaborately suspended muslin, and what do you end up with? A bare pot's bottom of precious liquid, dotted with suicidally greedy ants and bugs.

This is the smarter alternative: if you're feeling domestically inclined you can use it to glaze fruit tarts or to sweeten and perfume apple pies and crumbles; if not, then use it as a stickily aromatic sauce over good bought ice cream (and over lemon or lemon meringue ice cream it's superb) or dribble in coral wreaths over cream-splodged meringues.

1 quince **750g caster sugar**
750ml water **1 x 350ml jar**

Roughly chop the quince (a cleaver is probably the best tool for this), put the pieces – peel, pips and all – in a medium-sized saucepan with the water and sugar, and bring to the boil. Let it bubble away for a good hour, or until the liquid seems reduced by half, and strain into the prepared jar, in which you can keep it pretty indefinitely in the fridge.

Makes 350ml.

CURDS

Strictly speaking, a curd is not a larder item because it needs to be kept in the fridge, but that's irrelevant to my thesis: making a fruit curd is one of the simplest ways of making yourself feel like a provider of comforting domestic bounty.

CRANBERRY CURD

There is only one word to describe the colour of this fabulous, astringent but velvety curd: magenta. Well, some would say cerise, but that, of course, would convey quite the wrong culinary connotations. Either way, you get the picture.

I've given enough quantities to make quite a bit, because it occurs to me that it would make a good Christmas present.

500g cranberries
200ml water
100g unsalted butter

500g caster sugar
6 large eggs
5 x 250ml jars or equivalent

Place the cranberries and water in a saucepan, cover them and cook on a low heat until tender and popped. Pass the cranberries through a food mill (or push through a sieve) and put the fruit purée back into a saucepan. Add the butter and sugar, melting them gently. Beat the eggs in a bowl and sieve them into the saucepan. Stir the curd constantly over a medium heat until it has thickened. This requires patience as you don't want to speed things up and curdle the mixture, but that's not particularly challenging. When it has thickened, it should coat the back of a spoon. Let cool a little before pouring into the jars. Keep in the fridge.

Makes 1¼ litres.

PASSIONFRUIT CURD

As wonderful as this is to eat piled on top of fresh white bread, it is exceptional sandwiching a Victoria sponge, dolloped over muffins and pancakes, or poured into a cooked and cooled pastry case.

11 passionfruit
2 large eggs
2 large egg yolks

150g caster sugar
100g unsalted butter
1 x 350ml jar

Put the seeded pulp of 10 of the passionfruit into the processor and blitz just to loosen the seeds. Strain into a jug or bowl.

Beat the eggs, egg yolks and sugar together.

Melt the butter over a low heat in a heavy-based pan, and when melted stir in the sugar-egg mixture and the passionfruit juice, and keep cooking gently, stirring constantly, until thickened.

Off the heat, whisk in the pulp – seeds and all – of the remaining passionfruit, let cool slightly, then pour into the jar. Keep in the fridge.

Makes 350ml.

LIME CURD

Flora Woods gave me this recipe when she blessed me with her famous courgette cake (pp18–19). I'll pass on your thanks to her.

75g unsalted butter
3 large eggs
75g caster sugar
125ml lime juice (of approximately
  4 limes)

zest of 1 lime
1 x 350ml jar

Melt the butter in a heavy-based saucepan, add all the other ingredients and whisk to a custard over a gentle heat. Let cool before filling a jar – or a cake – with it. Keep in the fridge.

Makes 350ml.

Clockwise from top left: pink-grapefruit marmalade, greengage jam (p348) and soft-set peach and redcurrant jam (p349)

PINK-GRAPEFRUIT MARMALADE

Please note the easy method for making this: no muslin bags or funny business with suspended cheesecloths involved.

2 pink grapefruit, weighing
  approximately 800g
1kg preserving sugar

juice of 2 lemons
3 x 350ml jars or equivalent

Place a saucer in the deep freeze.

Put the pink grapefruit into a large saucepan, fill with enough water so that they float freely, bring to the boil and simmer for about 2 hours, by which time the grapefruit should be very soft. Add more hot water from a kettle if the liquid's boiling away.

Drain, remove the fruit to a board and slice the cooked grapefruit thinly, and then chop a bit, using the whole fruit, pith and all (though remove any large pips). Put the grapefruit back into the saucepan, and add the sugar and lemon juice. Let the sugar dissolve over a gentle heat and then bring to the boil until setting point is reached, about 15 minutes.

Ladle into prepared jars and close the lids.

Makes just over 1 litre.

VARIATIONS

To make ordinary orange marmalade, boil the same weight of Seville oranges for the same amount of time. When they're cooked and soft, take them out of the pan, reserving the liquid, cut them in half, scoop out the pips and put in a small pan, then chop up the oranges as finely or coarsely as you like and put them into a large pan.

Ladle some of the orange-cooking water over the pips in the small pan and put on the heat, bring to the boil and let boil for 5 minutes. Strain this over the chopped oranges in their pan, add the juice of 2 lemons and stir in 1.4kg sugar. Bring to the boil gently, so that the sugar dissolves before the jam actually starts boiling and then proceed as above.

To make ginger-orange marmalade, add about 1cm's worth of finely sliced or chopped ginger to the pips, and then push through 3cm's worth of ginger, in batches, through a garlic press to extract the juice over the pan of chopped oranges. Taste when you've reached setting point to see if you want to add more squeezed ginger.

I also love marmalade which is dark and treacly and especially aromatic: replace half the sugar with light muscovado (and add 1 tablespoonful of black treacle if you like this really dark) and pour in a slug of rum or bourbon, once with the chopped oranges and again after setting point is reached.

PICKLED PLUMS

If you go into some health stores or specialist shops you will find Japanese plum seasoning. It's an intensely sharp, clear pink plum (*ume*) vinegar. It seemed obvious, therefore, to use this to pickle plums. Quite apart from how good these taste, they look so beautiful, the dark red of the fruit in the tawny pink of the pickling liquid.

Bring out to eat with cold meats and use within 3–4 months, not because they'll go off but because after a while the fruit goes a bit too mushy.

500ml Japanese red-plum seasoning
375g caster sugar
2 star anise
25g fresh ginger, peeled and thinly
   sliced

1 tablespoon coriander seeds
2 cinnamon sticks, broken in half
3 strips of finely peeled orange zest
500g plums, halved and stoned
3 x 500ml jars or equivalent

In a large saucepan, bring the Japanese plum seasoning to the boil with the sugar, star anise, ginger, coriander seeds, cinnamon sticks and orange zest. Stir well until all the sugar has dissolved and simmer for 15 minutes, then take off the heat and allow to cool a little.

Pack the plum halves into the sterilized jars, to come within 5cm of the top, while the jars are still warm. Now pour the vinegar over, covering the plums by about 2½cm. Tap the jars to make sure there are no air bubbles, then insert a long skewer down the sides of the jars to double-check (this works on the swizzle-stick principle, or so I like to think). Make sure the spices and orange zest are fairly evenly shared out and arranged so as to maximize aesthetic pleasure. Seal the jars well, and store in a cool, dark place for at least a week before eating. Keep in the fridge once opened.

Makes 3 x 500ml jars.

VARIATION
Use red-wine vinegar (or any other vinegar you want) in place of the red-plum seasoning.

Clockwise from top: pineapple chutney (p358), spiced apple chutney and Chinese plum sauce (p363)

CHUTNEYS AND PICKLES

Chutneys, you should know before reading further, are a breeze to make. You simply chuck everything in one pan and let it boil for about 30 minutes until you've got a pulpy mass.

SPICED APPLE CHUTNEY

Well, all chutneys contain spices, but the intense, hot flavours in this chutney are the focus. I sneered when Hettie suggested this when we had a tree full of apples that I was letting rot, but she was right. The idea of apple chutney may seem unappealing – I just thought of it as grainy mush – but the taste is out of this world. I now cannot eat a Cornish pasty without it.

500g cooking apples
1 medium onion
2 bird's-eye red chillies
250g demerara sugar
1 teaspoon ground allspice
1 teaspoon ground cloves
1/2 teaspoon sea salt

black pepper
1 heaped tablespoon chopped or
grated fresh ginger
1 teaspoon turmeric
350ml cider vinegar
4 x 250ml jars or equivalent

Peel and roughly chop the apples, and finely chop the onion. Seed the chillies and chop them finely (I'd advise you to put on washing-up gloves for this, especially if you wear contact lenses).

Put all the ingredients in a pan, and bring to the boil. Cook over a medium heat for 30–40 minutes, until the mixture thickens. Spoon into the cleaned jars and, when cool, place them, with great and warm satisfaction, in your store cupboard.

Makes 1 litre.

EDITH AFIF'S LIME PICKLES

I call these lime pickles because that's what my friend Steve, who gave me this recipe of his late mother's, calls them. But think, rather, of limes, salted, rinsed and preserved in aromatic oil. When the Edith of the title made these in her native Egypt, she dredged the limes with salt over days; only later did she adapt her method to what was then modern technology. People can get so precious about tradition that I love the proof that change and modernity can be progress: somehow, salting the limes and leaving them in the deep freeze – rather brilliant of her to come up with the idea – breaks down the fruit's fibres much more effectively.

You either have a sour tooth or you don't. I do, and love these pickles – with bread and cheese, aromatic stews, cold meats, anything.

10 limes
1kg coarse salt
approximately 500ml olive oil (not extra virgin)
1 tablespoon turmeric

1 teaspoon cumin seeds
3 dried red chilli peppers, crumbled
3 x 350ml preserving jars
30 x 20cm baking tray or Pyrex dish

Cut the limes into eighths lengthways and cover the bottom of your dish with them. Cover the limes with the salt and then put in the freezer overnight or for a day (12 hours should do it, but longer won't hurt).

Remove from the deep freeze and thaw thoroughly. Put into a colander and rinse under the cold tap. Shake dry. Put a third into each clean, waiting jar. Decant the oil into a measuring jug and stir in the turmeric, cumin seeds and crumbled pepper. Pour the oil to come to the very top of the jars (and if you need more than 500ml to do this then simply add more – if the limes aren't submerged you'll get mould). Close and put away in a dark place. Leave for at least 3 weeks before eating. The longer you leave them, the more tender and exquisite they are.

Makes 3 x 350ml jars.

BROWN SAUCE

I know that the ingredients that follow hardly look like the stock constituents of brown sauce, and I should own up and say that this didn't start off life as brown sauce. It was conceived to be a rhubarb chutney, only I added too much liquid and what with one thing and another, I decided the only way to salvage it was to whizz it in the blender and turn it into a sauce. This isn't just a case of making the best of a bad lot: this is one of my favourite recipes in the whole book – for its depth of flavour, its full-toned tanginess – and a reminder that cooking is often about what you do, unplanned, in response to the here and now, not merely the careful application of culinary formulae.

1kg rhubarb

500g red onions (about 5 small ones)

2 long red chillies, deseeded

2 garlic cloves

300g cooking apple (about 1 medium)

30g (about 3cm) fresh ginger, minced

1 tablespoon ground ginger

1 tablespoon paprika

150g sultanas

75g dried cherries

500ml red-wine vinegar

1 tablespoon salt

1kg demerara sugar

2 x 1-litre jars and 1 x 500ml jar, or equivalent

Trim the rhubarb, chop it very roughly, put it into the food processor and chop finely, but don't turn it into a mush; you may want to do this in stages, or else just cut the trimmed rhubarb into ½cm slices by hand. Tip the chopped rhubarb into a large, heavy-bottomed pan. Now process the onions, chillies and garlic until finely chopped and transfer these to the pan with the rhubarb. Chop the apple the same way and add to the pan.

Stir in the minced fresh ginger (I use my fine Microplane grater which is peerless for this, but a garlic press would do just fine), the ground ginger, paprika, sultanas, dried cherries, red-wine vinegar, salt and sugar.

Bring to a boil, then lower the heat and simmer until everything has turned to an undulating but still just nubbly pulp – about 45 minutes.

Take the pan off the heat, let cool for about 10 minutes and then, a ladleful or so at a time, liquidize or process until smooth. Pour into the sterilized jars, let cool, cover and store away, with joy and satisfaction in your heart.

Makes 2½ litres.

CHINESE PLUM SAUCE

Whether people from China would call this a Chinese plum sauce I can't honestly say, but let's not quibble about details. It's wonderful with pork, with sharp Cheddar, with, well, most things. And sometimes I stir a tablespoon or two of it into a winey beef stew while I'm making it. It's very addictive, which I guess has something to do with both the sugar and the chilli – and the fact that it tastes so good.

I made it last year from some plums in my garden, which was particularly satisfying, but it's certainly worth buying some expressly for this.

2kg plums, stoned and quartered
750g apples, peeled, cored and cut into 1cm chunks
1 medium red onion
4 cloves of garlic, minced
750ml rice vinegar
500g caster sugar
500g dark muscovado sugar (or light if you prefer)
2cm piece of ginger, peeled and sliced into fine splinters

2 long red chillies
2–4 dried red chillies (depending on how hot you want it), crumbled
2 teaspoons ground Chinese 5-spice
1 stick of cinnamon, broken into pieces
2 pieces dried orange peel, optional
5 x 550ml jars

Use a big pan, such as a preserving pan, so that it can boil well to reduce, and put all the ingredients in it.

Cook everything at a steady boil for 1–1½ hours. When it is ready, it will still be runny – remember it is sauce – but it will become firmer; both the apples and the plums will set more on cooling. However, it should have reduced to make a jam-like mixture with no obvious signs of the fruit still apparent.

Bottle in the sterilized jars.

Makes 2¾ litres.

BIBLIOGRAPHY

Anderson, Pam, *The Perfect Recipe* (Houghton Mifflin, 1998)

Appel, Jennifer, and Allysa Torey, *The Magnolia Bakery Cookbook* (Simon & Schuster, 1999)

Bauer, Michael and Fran Irwin (eds), *The San Francisco Chronicle Cookbook* (Chronicle Books, 1997)

Bery, Odette J., *Another Season Cookbook* (The Globe Pequot Press, 1986)

Collister, Linda, *Sweet Pies and Tarts* (Ryland Peters & Small, 1997)

Colwin, Laurie, *Home Cooking* (HarperCollins, 2000)

Conte, Anna del, *The Gastronomy of Italy* (Bantam Press, 1987)

—— *Secrets from an Italian Kitchen* (Bantam Press, 1989)

Costa, Margaret, *Four Seasons Cookbook* (Grub Street, 1996)

Crawford-Poole, Shona, *Iced Delights* (Conran Octopus, 1986)

Farrow, Genevieve, and Diane Dreher, *The Joy of Muffins* (Golden West, 1989)

Fobel, Jim, *Jim Fobel's Old-Fashioned Baking Book: Recipes from an American Childhood* (Lake Isle Press, 1996)

Greenspan, Dorie, with Julia Child, *Baking with Julia* (William Morrow, 1996)

Greenstein, George, *Secrets of a Jewish Baker* (The Crossing Press, 1993)

Grigson, Jane, *Fruit Book* (Michael Joseph, 1982)

—— *English Food* (Ebury Press, 1992)

Kimball, Christopher, *The Yellow Farmhouse Cookbook* (Little, Brown, 1998)

Lawson, Nigella, *How to Eat* (Chatto & Windus, 1998)

Levy Beranbaum, Rose, *The Cake Bible* (William Morrow, 1988)

Machlin, Edda Servi, *The Classic Cuisine of the Italian Jews* (Giro Press, 1981)

McNair, James, *James McNair's Cakes* (Chronicle Books, 1999)

Ojakangas, Beatrice A., *The Great Scandinavian Baking Book* (University of Minnesota Press, 1999)

Ortiz, Joe, *The Village Baker* (Ten Speed Press, 1993)

—— and Gayle Ortiz, *The Village Baker's Wife* (Ten Speed Press, 1997)

Purdy, Susan G., *The Family Baker* (Broadway Books, 1999)

Rubinstein, Helge, *The Chocolate Book* (Macdonald & Co., 1981)

Schloss, Andrew, *One-Pot Cakes* (William Morrow, 1995)
Stavroulakis, Nicolas, *The Cookbook of the Jews of Greece* (Jason Aronson Inc., 1996)

Treuille, Eric and Ursula Ferrigno, *Bread* (Dorling Kindersley, 1998)

Willan, Anne, *Real Food: Fifty Years of Good Eating* (Macmillan, 1988)
Willard, Pat, *Pie Every Day* (Algonquin Books of Chapel Hill, 1997)
Wood, Beryl, *Let's Preserve It* (Souvenir Press, 1970)

ACKNOWLEDGEMENTS

There are many people who have helped, either with ingredients or equipment, in the course of this book, and to whom I owe thanks, most notably the Conran Shop, Ecko Bakeware, Graham & Greene, Kitchen Ideas, Marks & Spencer together with W. Brice and Son of Mockbeggar Farm, Michanicou Brothers, Mortimer & Bennett, Selfridges, Somerill & Bishop, Tiffany & Co., Vessel and Wedgwood.

One wanders into the land of platitude in saying that no book is the product of only one person's effort, but it's true all the same. I am grateful to a number of people, Eugenie Boyd, Caz Hildebrand, Gail Rebuck, Alison Samuel, Petrina Tinslay and Ed Victor chief among them.

I could not even broach the subject of my own, overwhelming gratitude without mentioning my three graces: those domestic goddesses Lisa Grillo and Kate Mellor, who have made it possible for me to work, to write, indeed to live, and Hettie Potter, who came into my life at just the right time, and without whom this book could never have been written. She has cooked with me, taken notes for me, supported me and kept me sane.

INDEX